THE SPIRIT OF GLORY

THE SPIRIT OF GLORY

by
F. W. DRAKE

Cathedral of St. James Library
South Bend, Indiana

LONGMANS, GREEN AND COMPANY
NEW YORK • LONDON • TORONTO

LONGMANS, GREEN AND CO., INC.
119 WEST 40TH ST., NEW YORK 18

LONGMANS, GREEN AND CO., LTD.
48 GROSVENOR STREET, LONDON W. 1

LONGMANS, GREEN AND CO.
20 CRANFIELD ROAD, TORONTO 16

THE SPIRIT OF GLORY

COPYRIGHT 1961
BY
LONGMANS, GREEN & CO., INC.

ALL RIGHTS RESERVED, INCLUDING THE RIGHT TO REPRODUCE
THIS BOOK, OR ANY PORTION THEREOF, IN ANY FORM

PUBLISHED SIMULTANEOUSLY IN THE DOMINION OF CANADA BY
LONGMANS, GREEN AND CO., TORONTO

AUTHORIZED EDITION

LIBRARY OF CONGRESS CATALOG CARD NUMBER 61-13442

Printed in the United States of America

PREFACE

This book of meditations on the Holy Spirit and His work in human life is meant to recall the inspiring power of His ministry in the simple daily round of every Christian life. When work presses heavily, as it does today, on men and women in all walks of life, and few are exempt from the tasks of Martha, it is all the more needful that we should guard the spirit of Mary, and be able to call to our help the glory which the Spirit of God reveals in the familiar scenes of daily work and daily prayers. To show how practical the belief in the Holy Spirit is, how necessary a part He plays in every full human life, how grievous is the loss of power and of joy where He is forgotten, how continuous is His secret work in all the interests and relations of ordinary life, how simple, how definite, and how fruitful are the normal methods of His consecrating grace, how bright and radiant is the life which owns the sway of the Spirit—that is the purpose of these meditations.

They are divided into sections which may be convenient for daily reading, and the prayers suggest the way in which we can learn to sum up the lessons of our reading, and come with our own offering of prayer and praise into the presence of God.

—F.W.D.

Contents

	Preface	v
I	Prologue	1
II	Glory	4
III	The Spirit of Jesus	15
IV	Holiness	26
V	Sacrifice	34
VI	Sympathy	47
VII	Comfort	59
VIII	Sacrament	70
IX	The Holy Eucharist	83
X	Ministry	96
XI	Fellowship	104

THE SPIRIT OF GLORY

I

Prologue

WHERE there is life there is growth. It is assumed too often that growth must be always uniform, ordered, and secure in its development. That is not, however, the lesson of nature. In nature growth is continuous, but life moves forward by sudden starts and bounds. After slow, secret processes of preparation comes a sudden outburst of glory and beauty. Special seasons give stirring impulse to all the forces of life, and the achievement of a few days rivals the growth of months. So it is with the spiritual life. There are seasons of intensity and periods of crisis when, under the vital impulse of the Spirit, the soul makes sudden advance, blossoms into new beauty, and attains unexpected glory. The difficulties of long months of slow progress are overcome and God astonishes the soul with the seeming ease and rapidity of its advance.

It may be that such a time is the season when this book is taken up. Whether it be Lent or any time of special retreat, or a succession of quiet moments stolen out of the pressure of a very busy life, or whenever we study the ways of the Spirit of Glory and of God, the method is the same. Little seasons of stillness and study are like locks upon the river of life—locks that keep the stream from rushing headlong and useless to the sea, and make long

The Spirit of Glory

levels and quiet reaches where boats go to and fro, and men can rest and work and play.

With the opening of a book, the lock gates open wide. In we slip under the shadow of the grey-green walls. The gates shut behind us. The outer world is withdrawn, and we see only the narrow limits of the lock and the blue sky above. The sluice gates open, and the water comes bubbling and eddying about us. We have enough to do at first to keep the boat-head straight. As the waters rise, the sluices open wider, but the wild rush and tumble of the tide is done. Soon the swelling water raises us to the full height of the upper levels of the stream. We glance at the old level below, and as the gates quietly swing open and out, we glide into the upper waters.

So in such a season or time as this we are raised upon the tide of grace to the higher levels of life. At first, as the gates close in upon us, we may be confused at the restraint, the narrowed outlook, the first eddying perils of the rushing waters. Slowly come peace and calm as we rise upon the tide. At last in quiet and in hope we move into the flowing stream, borne now upon a higher tide of grace, seeking the Source of Life and bound for God.

So may the quiet times spent in this study of the Holy Ghost the Comforter bring us nearer to God and touch our lives anew with the glory of His presence and His power.

A PRAYER FOR THE HOLY SPIRIT

O Holy Spirit, lord of life and font of truth, who hast made our bodies thy temple and our souls thy home; Grant that day by day we may submit ourselves to thy

Prologue

guidance, rejoice in thy truth and respond in all things to the inspiration of thy holiness, who with the Father and the Son livest and reignest God for ever and ever. Amen.

II

Glory

"The spirit of glory and of God resteth upon you." The context shows that St. Peter regards this as a source of confidence to the Christian, which enables him to do his work, to bear his witness, and to be worthy of the name of Christ, even in the "fiery trial" of suffering and persecution. "If ye are reproached for the name of Christ, blessed are ye, for the spirit of glory and of God resteth upon you." Perhaps we too could gain that serenity of heart, that steadfast assurance, and that winning habit of content, which are still the unfailing witness of the true Christian life, if we were more conscious that God is ever waiting to fill our lives with glory and to make them rich with the endowment of His Spirit. How little we think of that glory as the common possession of our everyday life, the constant aim of our endeavors, the hidden factor in all our successes, the point of our beginning and the end of our race!

In one of her "revelations of divine love" Julian of Norwich relates how once, as she walked through the woods, she picked up a hazel-nut from the ground and, laying it in the palm of her hand, saw in that little thing "three properties. The first is that God made it, the second is that God loveth it, the third that God keepeth it."

Glory

So it is that God Almighty is the creator, lover and keeper also of the soul of man. Perhaps it is in this last work of guardianship and protection and consecration that the Holy Ghost shows Himself peculiarly the Spirit of Glory.

As the Spirit of Glory, the Holy Ghost is not only Himself glorious, but He is the giver of glory. For it is the characteristic of God that all His attributes are instinct with will. God is not only Himself eternally holy, stainless, and pure, but aflame with eager zeal to create holiness in all His creatures. Not only are all the treasures of wisdom and knowledge hid in God, but He is eternally active to reveal and disseminate that wisdom and that knowledge. So the Holy Spirit is not merely glorious, shining with the spiritual splendor of eternal majesty and perfect beauty, but He bestows, imparts, and achieves glory wherever He dwells. St. Basil acknowledges this when he says that all things yearn for Him, that aim at excellence.

We should try to understand what is meant by glory. Glory is ultimate and absolute perfection. The glory of a person is the achievement of his true destiny, the crown of his life's endeavor. The glory of a thing is the exact fulfillment of the purpose for which it was made. The glory of a watch would consist not in the beauty of its case, however rich and costly, but in its perfection of timekeeping. It is the work of the Holy Ghost to lead man to the complete achievement of God's eternal purpose. Nothing therefore can be more practical and less doctrinaire than the study of the influence of the Holy Spirit upon the activities of human life.

The Spirit of Glory

[A]

Nothing so effectually lays our spiritual life in ruins as ignorance or neglect of the Person and work of the Holy Spirit. The commonest errors of belief which are in vogue today may be traced to a misunderstanding of the work of the Holy Spirit.

If, for instance, men cannot rise beyond the narrow creed of a stark mechanism, in which matter is divorced from all alliance with spirit, in which there is no place for sacrament because no interplay is possible between the material and the spiritual, it is because they do not understand that the world is not merely created by God, but it is ever God-inspired and God-possessed. They have no knowledge of the eternal Spirit of Life immanent in all created things.

It is the same with the cult of Christian Science. Surely no school of thought was ever more oddly named. With its denial of the central truth of Christian creeds—the reality of the Incarnation, it shows itself incapable of the name of Christian, while its equivocations and fluid inability of exact definition make it a travesty of science. When you ask why some men and women feel bound to deny the reality of all they see or do, and declare that they live in a world of illusion, you find it is because they do not know that it is the eternal Spirit of God who gives reality both to the human nature of the Incarnate and to the experiences of our human life today.

In a similar way, whenever men seek refuge in Spiritualism that they may find fellowship with the departed, it is because they have not known the working of the divine

Glory

Spirit of Holiness, who is the only stable and abiding bond of fellowship in human life, leaping the barriers of time and space, as He links all souls in one unbroken communion, the mediator alike of their individual religious experience and of the unity of their common life.

When men have been attracted by the specious theories which make men gods and call them Christs, it has been because they have not realized the essential distinction between the divine nature of the indwelling Spirit and the created nature of man in whom He dwells so quietly. They have claimed identity where God has decreed fellowship. Man can be godlike through the power of the Spirit, but God he can never be.

So it is ignorance of the Spirit of Glory that blinds men to the realities of life and to the close intimacies of God with the souls which He has made.

[B]

It is the glory of the Spirit that He not only "searcheth all things, yea, the deep things of God," but He also shows us the things of Jesus and enables us rightly to know what is in man.

The Holy Spirit is more than the revealer of the Glory of God. The reverent mind can conceive Him in a very real way. The Holy Spirit Himself completes and fulfills the divine glory. For in the relations of the Blessed Trinity, as we are allowed to figure them humbly to ourselves, it is the Spirit who gives perfection and adds fulfillment to the eternal mystery of Almighty God. He is the bond of the Trinity, mediating that mutual love which

The Spirit of Glory

links the Three eternally in One, the blessed harmony of Father and of Son, the fellowship, the common life of both.

As the Spirit crowns the glory of the divine Being, so also He constitutes the glory of all created life and ensures to every creature the fulfillment of its purpose. Each act of God's creation finds its perfection attained through the work of the Spirit. He gives life and actuality to what the Father performs through the Son. So it is, in the words of the Book of Wisdom, that "the Spirit of the Lord hath fulfilled the world" and "holdeth all things together." In the work of final achievement and perfecting of all things He "reacheth from one end of the world to the other with full strength and ordereth all things graciously." It was in the plentitude of the Spirit's life-giving power that "God saw everything that He had made, and, behold, it was very good."

If we may thus speak with reverent truth of the Spirit's work of glory in the Godhead and in all creation, how much more clearly may we recognize His work in that perfection of human life which belongs to the Incarnate Son. It was God's purpose according to the terms of man's creation that his destined fellowship with God should come by the gift of the Holy Spirit, and that it should be the Spirit's part to ensure that conformity to the image of God which is man's characteristic glory. God could only look upon human life as complete in the consecrating and fulfilling power of the indwelling Spirit. So we can understand how for the fullness of His human perfection Jesus availed Himself of the endowment of the Holy Spirit. As we watch the growth of Jesus, we see

Glory

Him fulfilling the ideal of human childhood, youth, and manhood, lacking nothing at each stage for the complete development of mind and character proper to that condition. "The child grew and waxed strong" in the power of the Spirit. All through the silences of the thirty years of retreat it was the Holy Ghost who equipped Him for the tasks of the carpenter's shop and sustained His human soul in communion with the Father. When His "hour" was come and the toils of His public ministry began, it was "in the power of the Spirit" that He taught, and "with the finger of God" that His miracles were performed, and at length it was "through the eternal Spirit" that He "offered Himself without spot to God." So the glory of that perfect human life in all its manifold experiences of suffering, agony, and grief was achieved in the power of the Holy Spirit.

The great legacy of Christ to His Church was the gift of the same Spirit, so that we too in our own manhood might be strengthened for all the duties of life. It is the Spirit's work, according to the loving purpose of Christ, to fulfill the mission of the Incarnation and to achieve a manhood redeemed from sin and restored to holy fellowship with God. It is, as Julian says, "by the blissful touching of the Holy Ghost," by "our good Lord, the Holy Ghost, which is endless life dwelling in our soul," that all the natural yearnings of the soul are sated and we come to God in our helplessness, "simply and plainly and humbly," sustained through all our pilgrimage by "the soft comfort of the Holy Ghost." So does the Spirit of Glory fulfill His work as the faithful keeper of the souls of men.

The Spirit of Glory

[C]

In what ways will that glory reveal itself in the lives of us, who are but ordinary men and women, with no unusual spiritual powers or aspirations, immersed in the constant drudgery of many an unromantic task, absorbed in the ceaseless round of unremitting toil? Is there fruit of the Spirit which we can gather? In three ways at least all of us can bring joy and strength into our lives by acceptance of the Spirit's timely help.

His presence spreads through the life a spirit of repose. If God wills that "we be secure in love and restful and peaceable as He is," it is the Spirit's indwelling that brings us that serenity of heart. The sense of sonship which the Spirit creates, whereby we cry, Abba, Father, sustains us in quiet reliance upon the will of God. "Ye have an unction from the Holy One and know all things." An unquestioned assurance, born of the Spirit's inspiration, stills our restless striving. We breathe that calm air of naive trust which marked the filial attitude of Jesus as He fulfilled the will of the Father. "The perfection of happiness," says Lacordaire, "is to know how to abandon oneself." To yield ourselves fully to the vocation of the Holy Ghost is to achieve tranquillity, to gain that peace which no man taketh from us. If in the midst of our tumultous life we would find rest, we cannot give ourselves too freely to the leading of the Holy Spirit, who will work in us, who will pray in us, not as we will, but as He intends. It is not the slothful repose of a studied inactivity, but the calm rest of a soul that knows in

Glory

whom it has believed, that casts its burden upon the Lord and follows where He calls.

Out of the heart of that repose the Spirit of Glory wakes in us a response—a response to the love of Jesus on whom our hearts are stayed. As the soul gazes in serene faith upon the heart of God unveiled in the life of Jesus and interpreted to us in the voiceless whispers of the Spirit, heart speaks to heart, and the call of the Beloved rouses the generous response of a life that knows itself redeemed, "bought with a price" that none but God could pay. So there springs up that active intercourse of man with God, which moves forward in ever-renewed cycle of prayer and service, service and vision, vision and communion, till all the energies of life are drawn into constant and joyous reaction to the love of God.

When that response tires and the spirit of man grows weary, beset by the toils and temptations that befall us in the way, the Spirit achieves His final glory in our fallen life by reviving our soul with the energies of a divine renewal. He is the one who pours new vigor and vitality into our hearts, and enriches us with gifts of abounding life. Men of deep religious experience, like Suso and Pascal, have in this renewing power of the Spirit received a quickening of spiritual life which seemed no less than a "second conversion." What God has given, God alone can keep, God alone can renew, God alone can lead to perfection. The work of God in the life, this daily work, is the task of the Holy Spirit. There is no simpler and no surer way to growth in holiness than a fresh surrender every day to the renewing energies of the Spirit's

The Spirit of Glory

consecration. If it is true, as Bossuet says, that whoever loves Jesus is always beginning over again, it is in the power of the Spirit of Glory that the new beginning is perpetually made. God does not ask us to make victories, but to do our best. To begin the day with the resolve that by the grace of the Spirit we will do our best to recall through the day, in moments of need and stress, of ease and of joy, His indwelling presence, to close the day with an act of penitence for our forgetfulness of His help and a thanksgiving for every remembrance of His aid—to do that is to realize how rich the life may grow which trusts the unfolding of its glory to the "heavenly assistance of the Holy Ghost."

[D]

The way in which the Spirit leads us from glory to glory, as stage succeeds stage in the normal development of our religious life, may be typified by the very ground plan of the parish church in which we worship. Born in the world we stand, as it were, at the west end of some great church. Our eyes travel up the nave and rest at length on the beauty of the sanctuary, where the east end glows with the glory of mullioned window or the splendor of tapestry, carving, or picture, where the altar of friendship stands, where we meet God and He meets us in Holy Communion. That indeed is our goal—communion with God, and life's task is to find that fellowship. That is the end God has set before us.

As we move forward in the church, we come at once to the font and make the first step in our pilgrimage. There

Glory

God waits to bless us with the gift of the Holy Spirit. There is our first experience of how God makes us equal to our task. God takes the soul into His keeping, and while it is yet unconscious of any power of response, the Spirit shapes and moulds and fashions it from within, and guides it on its way to God.

With our heart still set upon fellowship with God, we move up the aisle till we come to the chancel steps which lead into the choir. There sits the bishop, waiting to lay his hands upon us, to confirm us with the full strength of the Spirit, to consecrate all our faculties in the service and work to which God has called us.

We go forward now to the altar, and there, kneeling to greet our Blessed Lord at His coming, we begin a life of fellowship, which is a real entrance upon a heavenly life. There a window is opened into heaven and the worship of earth is crowned with the advent of God. In the steadfastness of Eucharistic fellowship we attain the fullness of glory of which this life is capable. When death comes to find us still kneeling in our place before the altar, it is just as though the bright east wall fell away before us, and we passed through the familiar glory of the earthly sanctuary to a new glory of closer fellowship—a deeper and richer fellowship, a new fellowship but not a strange one, because the Spirit has brought us thus far Himself. The same Spirit who has led us by sacramental ways to the glory of God in this life will lead us beyond. If His gifts have been sure and fruitful here, they will be yet more prized and more abundant there. "After the Resurrection," said St. Cyril of Alexandria, "the divine Spirit will be in us, not in installments nor by measure,

The Spirit of Glory

but richly and abundantly, and we shall perfectly luxuriate in the gifts that are ours through Christ." So the path of glory leads beyond the grave to the fulfillment of human life in God. The one aim of life abides, fulfilled at length in the glory of the Spirit:

> For I intend to get to God,
> For 'tis to God I speed so fast,
> For in God's breast, my own abode,
> I lay my spirit down at last.

A PRAYER FOR PERFECTION

Holy Spirit of Glory and of God, proceeding from the Father and the Son, eternal bond of unity and love, by whom all creation lives and the whole body of the Church is sanctified; Supply, we beseech thee, every need and bring all to perfection, that the earth may be filled with the glory of the Lord, and that being knit eternally to thee we may be found faithful to our vocation and be made partakers of thy blessedness, who in the unity of the Father and the Son, livest and reignest God for ever and ever. Amen.

III

The Spirit of Jesus

"The spirit of glory and of God resteth upon you." Some people think that here St. Peter is using the word "glory" as a title of Jesus Christ, the Son of God, the Word of God made flesh. Whether or not that be so, the suggestion at least illustrates the unique relation which the Holy Spirit bears to Jesus Christ. The Spirit of God, as we know Him, is the Spirit of Jesus the Incarnate, and the Interpreter of Christ in our time and place.

[A]

Christianity is above all things a dispensation of the Holy Spirit. The work of Christ is continued and completed in the power of the Holy Spirit. At all stages the work of the Holy Spirit is inseparably associated with the person and work of Christ, so that the coming of the Holy Ghost completes the purpose for which God was revealed in Jesus Christ. The fellowship with God which the Incarnation inaugurated is attained and fulfilled for us in the ministry of the Holy Spirit. That is the express purpose of Christ, deliberately announced before the Crucifixion—the work which Jesus Himself had planned,

The Spirit of Glory

had outlined, and had begun during the years of His public ministry—that was the work which was to be developed, achieved, and consummated through the agency of the Holy Spirit. "These things have I spoken unto you, being yet present with you. But the Comforter, which is the Holy Ghost, whom the Father will send in my name, he shall teach you all things." "I will pray the Father, and he shall give you another Comforter, that he may abide with you for ever . . . the Spirit of truth." So it was that the Apostles could not begin to carry out the purposes of Christ until they had waited for the promise of the Father and had received power through the outpouring of the Holy Ghost at Pentecost. The Holy Spirit is not an episode, not an afterthought, in the purposes of Christ, but of the very essence of the creation and redemption of the whole world, past, present, and future, the very essence of Christ's work and kingdom.

[B]

To overlook the deliberate purpose of Christ to complete all in the Holy Spirit is to make a common misuse of the Gospels. Men often handle certain portions of the Gospel story as though they were the whole and entire record of the human life and work of Christ, whereas the larger part of the activities of the Incarnate Son will be found beyond this three years' ministry and outside the scope of the Gospel narrative. Wonderful indeed was the influence of those three years of Christ's public life. Lecky was undoubtably right in saying, "The simple record of three short years of active life has done more to

The Spirit of Jesus

regenerate and soften mankind than all the disquisitions of philosophers and all the exhortations of moralists." That is indeed true, but the actual work of regeneration through all the centuries is the very work of Him whose life of growing influence did not cease with three short years of visible ministry. The New Testament does not end with the Gospels, it begins with them, and it goes on with the story of Christ's work actually carried out, as He Himself had planned it, in the power of the Holy Spirit. The life and teaching of the risen and glorified Christ, which is the special fruit of the Spirit's work, mightily surpass in wonder and power all the marvels of His public ministry.

Christ Himself had promised that it should be so. His departure to the Father with the ensuing mission of the Holy Ghost was to be the opening of a more glorious scene in the drama of the Incarnation. "He that believeth on me, the works that I do shall he do also; and greater works than these shall he do; because I go unto My Father." The ministry of the Spirit is to be more splendid and more evident in its power than the ministry of those three years of Christ's incarnate life, just because it is the work of the same Christ, yet more mature, more fully developed, and seen on a wider stage. It is no wonder that those who confine their vision of the work of Christ to the bare Gospel narrative should easily forget that He is God and see in Him only man. They close their eyes to the greater part of His work. They see Him as a healer, teacher, and shepherd of souls; they see Him tempted and suffering, and victorious over sin and death. They need to study the Epistles and the Acts of the Apostles

The Spirit of Glory

to understand the full meaning of His divine Person and to see the true method of His saving work. Only then may they enter into the mystery of His mediation, His high-priestly life of intercession, and His supreme and universal Kingship. Only then may they see Christ as Head of the Church and Judge of the world, and then, and above all, see how the redeeming efficacy of His life and death is perpetually mediated to us today through the mission of the Holy Spirit. "He shall glorify me: for he shall receive of mine, and shall show it unto you." Jesus is not only Himself anointed by the Holy Spirit in the fullness of His own manhood, but it is the same Spirit with which He anoints us; He consummates His work in us by the gift of the Holy Spirit, poured forth upon us from the splendors of that manhood now ascended and glorified.

[C]

It is very easy to see in the Gospels that Jesus did not intend to complete His work in His earthly lifetime. He never ceased to talk about a universal kingdom; yet, as the disciples found to their continual perplexity and dismay, He took no effective steps to shape the kingdom and assume the sovereignty, even when the opportunity was thrust upon Him. The Galilean offer of kingship He refused. He withdrew the disciples in order that He might prepare them for the work of His Kingdom. He promised them the power of the Holy Spirit to carry on after His Ascension what He Himself had begun. He prepared the visible framework, He laid the plans and determined the

The Spirit of Jesus

laws of His kingdom, but it was by the power of the Holy Spirit that He founded it, and it was by the life of the Spirit that He gave it vitality and effective vigor to continue into our time and place.

As the Incarnation was definite and precise in its methods, expressing itself in outward and visible ways, so also was, and is, the way of the Holy Ghost, the Spirit of the Incarnate, definite in outward expression. The Holy Spirit came in a visible and clear way, and the society of the Church was visibly planted among men to be the home of the Spirit, His special organ and instrument for working upon and with and for mankind. A fellowship, a society was the natural method of the Spirit's working in human life, because it is only through social relations that the life of the individual can be developed. The Church therefore stands as the visible organ of the Spirit in the work of God among men, and the progress of the work of the Spirit is marked by visible sacramental agencies, definite, exact, and precise in their outward ordering and sure in their inward efficacy. The Holy Spirit sent by Christ is described by Jesus Himself as a second Paraclete, His second Self. From Baptism, through Confirmation to Communion, through Absolution and Unction, through Ordination and Consecration, the chain of the Holy Spirit's hallowing agency continues, ministering to us the life of God, transfiguring us into the very image of the Incarnate Son as he leads us from glory to glory.

The Spirit of Glory

[D]

Of the ministry of the Holy Spirit in the Church of Jesus Christ it may be said that the Spirit's primary work is to create, to maintain, and to develop the spiritual life. He is the source of all perfection and the object of all true desire. This is true of all spheres of life, both in nature and in human history. Above all must it be true in the perfection of that highest sphere of man's capacities and interests—the spiritual life, and man's desire for God. According to St. Augustine, "the whole life of a good Christian consists in holy desire." That fundamental desire, that yearning of the soul for God, that hunger and thirst after righteousness, is the creation and gift of the Spirit of Jesus. Behind all our failures in devotion, our lassitude in prayer, our irregular meditation, our frail and flickering consciousness of the presence and power of God, lies the primal want of a continuous and sufficient desire for spiritual things. We need a fuller and firmer grasp of the beauty of the heavenly life, of the reality of God, of the supreme attractiveness of all that is holy and good. Sometimes we think, as we go on day by day steadfastly observing the rules of the Church and continuing in the wonted ways of public and private devotion, that the love of holiness will grow naturally in us. We imagine that the long lapse of time and the cumulative influence of habit will of themselves deepen in us the strength of spiritual desire. Such a hope is belied by experience. Only the Spirit of God Himself can give us that desire for God, only the Spirit of Glory can maintain and develop it, and lead us ever upward in the love of all

The Spirit of Jesus

that is heavenly. It is He who quickens our desires with such a power of perseverance that the difficulties of the spiritual way are overcome by the kindling zeal of love. The conflicts of life can be endured, its temptations can be resisted, its suffering can be borne, because the end is made desirable by the revelation of the Spirit. For the Spirit, revealing to us Jesus, enables us to see life wholly and to see it clearly, and to view all things in the right proportion and perspective. He endows us with a power of divine vision which lays bare before our gaze the deep realities of life. Under His guidance we can discriminate between the specious importance of that which is worldly and the true value of that which is eternal. The eternal that lies hid in the temporal is revealed to our eyes. We see things as they truly are. From all that seems commonplace and dull, the veil is lifted and we see the gleam of the timeless and the eternal. The beauty that the world has for God Himself is seen through the eyes of the Spirit. That is the secret of the effective power of Christianity. It is a deeply spiritual religion, not because it withdraws men from the interests and work of daily life, but because it reveals the world as the sphere in which God is working, and claims for God all the highest energies of human effort and desire.

The spiritual life, however hard it may seem to our earliest experience, ceases to be so difficult when the Spirit enables us to think of it in a Godward manner. If the soul is to be athirst for God, it must be the Holy Ghost who, in the power of His secret indwelling, renews all the Godward impulses of the heart, and holds the will fast in loving obedience to the promptings of a pure

The Spirit of Glory

conscience. The Spirit rules and disciplines the affections, and the rule of the Spirit is found to be neither burden nor yoke, but a liberty of free and loving service, drawing all the interests of life together into a happy and zealous quest after holiness. God becomes our delight. His ways are understood, admired, and followed with growing gladness. We can persevere gladly with the drudgery of a task that apparently will yield nothing but failure, because the Spirit of the triumphant Christ shows us victory at the end. There is no despair where there is the inextinguishable hope of the Spirit. "I look for the Lord; my soul doth wait for him; in his word is my trust." That is the attitude of the Spirit-guided life.

[E]

When then we look once more at our devotional life and see its poverty, its inadequacy, its repeated failures, we may need to lean more faithfully upon the covenanted grace of the indwelling Spirit and to realize that it is He who can bring glory where there was shame, and joy where there was sadness; He alone creates in us the life of Jesus. St. Paul expresses the different attributes of the character of Christ which the Spirit forms in us as "the fruit of the Spirit"—love, joy, peace, long-suffering, gentleness, goodness, faith, meekness, temperance. It is impossible not to set the phrase of St. Paul "fruit of the Spirit" side by side with the words of our Lord, "I am the vine, ye are the branches. . . . The branch cannot bear fruit of itself, except it abide in the vine; no more can ye, except ye abide in me." This fruit is the result of our un-

The Spirit of Jesus

broken union with Christ, which the Spirit assures. The blessed Spirit is the sap of strength and vital energy which carries the life of Christ through all the branches, the safeguard of unity, and the source of fruitfulness. "Without me ye can do nothing."

Christian character is a growth of virtues from within, not a gradual building up by addition from without. This is the truth which William Wilberforce, the emancipator of slaves, put very clearly in a letter to his boy Samuel. "I will mention a striking illustration of the difference between men's striving to improve one or another, individual good quality, and improving the common root of them all and thereby improving them all at once. The former is the way in which the human artificer works, a statuary, for instance, sometimes making a finger, sometimes a leg, and so on, while the latter, the workmanship of the Divine Artificer, is like the growth of a plant or a tree in which all the various parts are swelling out and increasing, or, as we term it, growing, at the same time. . . . It teaches us a most important truth, that we should strive to obtain the heavenly principle of growth in grace and in goodness, by obtaining more of the Holy Spirit of God, and then we shall improve in every particular grace and virtue." The Spirit of Jesus enables us to become godlike, making it possible for us to reflect in our lives, however faintly, some of the attributes of His own incarnate life. It is God Himself, therefore, whom we must desire. Perhaps we do not pray because we have no wish to talk with God. The Bible is not read because we do not really want to know more about Christ and His Church. The will remains undisciplined because goodness is not in it-

The Spirit of Glory

self attractive and we do not have before us the divine ideal of holiness. Then is when we must arouse the gift of the Holy Ghost within us and claim the glory that is ours. He is the font of holiness and sanctification; He will refresh in us the spirit of devotion and help us to desire God. God has made us to love Him. Jesus has shown that God is lovable. The Spirit of Jesus, the indwelling Spirit of Glory, enables us to desire God to realize the love that God asks of us. The Spirit of God gives the soul an appetite for God and awakens in us an alert and eager expectation of God. It is therefore to the Holy Spirit that we need often to pray, for only by so doing can we fully know and appreciate His personality. The more difficult it is to realize the personality of the Holy Ghost, the more needful it is to turn to Him in prayer. "No creature," says St. Basil, "can dispense with the teaching and sanctifying power of the Spirit. The Holy Spirit enlightens the soul and makes it see what is beyond sight. Under His influence the soul mirrors the heavens while the body is still on earth. Man, little as he is, in the Spirit sees the beginning and the end of the world. He knows what he has never learned, for the true Illuminator is within."

Let us trust that Illuminator more faithfully as we set ourselves to prayer, for He will rally our thoughts and calm our souls and find words for our intercourse with God. The words may be of Holy Scripture, or of our own, or of some sermon we have recalled; use them as fuel for the fire of your devotion, till, as you muse, the flame is kindled and you find God. Our prayers would be greatly enriched if we resolved never to let any regular occasion of devotion pass without at least one simple in-

The Spirit of Jesus

vocation of the Holy Spirit or some act of praise and adoration in His name.

A PRAYER FOR CHRIST-LIKENESS

Holy and eternal Spirit, through whom Jesus offered himself without spot to God; Dwell in our hearts with power and show to us the things of Jesus, his glory, his pity, and his love, that by thy hallowing grace we may follow the blessed steps of his most holy life and be made in all things like unto Him, our Lord and Saviour Jesus Christ. Amen.

IV

Holiness

THERE is no glory in life without love. No word is more frequently on our lips and none perhaps more sadly misused than love. So little do we value love for its worth that few recognize in it the crowning proof of our response to the work of the Holy Spirit in our hearts; yet the love of which the New Testament speaks is always the love which the Spirit inspires: it is never the mere emotional impulse or instinctive desire, however pure, of unaided human nature. "The more excellent way" of St. Paul's rhapsody is that by which love is shed abroad in our hearts by the Spirit of God. Our love is the reflection of that divine image, which has been recreated in us in all its beauty of holiness by the Spirit of Glory.

[A]

We recognize in love the essential glory and eternal excellency of God. When we try to picture the mutual relationship of co-inhering love which marks the life of God, we think of the Holy Spirit as the bond of love in that divine fellowship. The eternal love of God is revealed to us in the sacred manhood of Jesus, the crown of the Spirit's work in all created life. The human life of

Holiness

Jesus is the prism in which we can see God. Just as the white light of the sun, as it flashes upon cut crystal or bevelled glass, is broken up into the varied colors of the rainbow, and figures of every hue dance before our eyes, so the light of the stainless glory of God is refracted through the manhood of Jesus, and is broken up into the manifold beauty of those varied attributes and perfections which our human eyes can distinguish and our minds can understand. In that way Jesus may be called the prism of God. The revelation of God in Jesus comes to the full at the Cross. It is in Jesus crucified that we have the most complete revelation of the love of God. There love is seen as holiness, sacrifice, and sympathy—glories of human life which we can appreciate and honor, values which we can apprehend and treasure and attain.

Love is holiness. When Jesus through the eternal Spirit offered Himself without spot to God, His offering of love was an offering of holiness—the offering by one who was Himself essentially and eternally holy, the offering of a human nature in which the Holy Spirit had achieved an unhindered work of perfect holiness. It is the holiness, not the suffering, that is of the essence of the Atonement. What pleased the Father was the spotless offering of a human life freely dedicated, even to death, to the vindication of the holiness of God. The fruit of the Spirit's perfect work in Jesus is seen in the stainless allegiance of His pure body and soul to the holy will of God. The prince of this world had nothing in Him. In revealing the heart of God, Jesus first revealed His holiness. The whole effort of Christ's ministry, the purpose of His miracles, the sum of His teaching, the meaning of His sacrifice—

The Spirit of Glory

all was the manifestation of a God whose love was grounded in holiness. The horror that weighed upon the soul of Jesus was the vision of man's sin; the joy that roused His spirit to happy thanksgiving and praise was the assertion of human goodness.

In revealing the holiness of God, Jesus did more than disclose the essential righteousness of the divine nature. Holiness applied to God is a term that has more than a moral significance: it not only expresses the fact that there is in God an absolute, inviolable, unchanging, essential standard of goodness, which is the guide and hope of all human life, but it also suggests the overplus of meaning which transcends morality, that something incomprehensible, that mystery and transcendent majesty, at once daunting and fascinating, which is the eternal attribute of Him "who is the blessed and only Potentate, the King of kings and Lord of lords; Who only hath immortality, dwelling in light which no man can approach unto; whom no man hath seen, nor can see." Jesus, in revealing God as Love, not only presented to man the vision of a God whose flawless purity is the measure of human goodness, but also disclosed a God whose holiness claims the adoring worship of all mankind. Our love, the fruit of the Spirit's indwelling, is at once the pledge of our holiness and the spring of our devotion.

[B]

It is the glory of the Spirit to create the holiness of Jesus in the lives of those who love God. What is holi-

Holiness

ness in the life of Jesus is penitence in ours. Penitence is the perfected glory of human love for a God who is worshipped as holy. Such love, with its inner vision of the divine beauty of holiness, can be shed abroad in our hearts only through the indwelling of the Holy Ghost.

The first step in that penitence is sincere and honest self-knowledge, and it is in the light of the Spirit that we take that first step. It is the gift of the Spirt that we have the vision of God—a vision which stirs the soul to aspirations of holiness and to discontent with our allowed imperfections; it is in the light of the Spirit's inspiration that we pledge ourselves to uncompromising sincerity, and are able to read our hearts without prejudice, presumption, or despair. After the Spirit has given us a sense of truth, we can see ourselves as we really are.

The next step in our endeavor after penitence is to acquire such a love of God that the knowledge of ourselves as we really are makes us grieve for the sorrow with which we wound the heart of Jesus. The Spirit, that moved the sinless human heart of Christ to grieve over man's sin, stirs in our sinful hearts a loathing for the stubbornness and pride and apathy that shame our discipleship and grieve our Lord. When Dante pictures the three steps that lead to the gate of pardon, the second step is described as "of a stone rugged and burnt, cracked in its length and breadth." This "godly sorrow" is also the Spirit's gift, and in no effort of our spiritual life must we yield ourselves more utterly to the leading of the Holy Ghost or be more content with the measure of His gift. Nowhere is the wise caution of the mystic Hylton more needful, "See thy feebleness and bear it patiently. Do

The Spirit of Glory

what belongs to thee and suffer our Lord to give what He wills and teach Him not."

The last step in penitence, which proves the sincerity of both our self-knowledge and our contrition, is that of confession and amendment. That means our detailed repudiation of what we know to be wrong—a self-abasement which tests at once our insight into our own hearts and our trust in the mercy of God—and it carries with it a definite resolve to put out of our lives all that we condemn, and to make a constant effort towards that ideal of goodness which we have seen afresh in our vision of the love and holiness of God. For the effort of amendment the Holy Spirit equips us with the grace of fortitude or "ghostly strength." The resolve made in the impulse of the Spirit at the moment of penitence with a full knowledge of the struggle which it will cost, must be renewed daily, not in our own power, but in serene reliance upon the enabling grace of the Holy Spirit.

Two things often mar the progress of our penitential life. Sometimes we have not the courage to accept the immeasurable wonder of God's forgiveness. It seems too splendid to be true. We need such a quickening of faith that we may be able to see ourselves as God sees us—accepted in the Beloved, forgiven through the cleansing blood of Jesus, robed in His righteousness—all unworthily but indubitably recreated in life and holiness. That there may be no uncertainty or indecision about the irrevocable fullness of our pardon, the Spirit provides for us the ministry of sacramental absolution.

God has not failed to furnish His Church with a ministry of holiness which shall assure to penitent souls the

Holiness

authoritative pardon of His absolving love. The very first breath of the Holy Spirit upon the Apostles was accompanied with the empowering words which Christ used to constitute the charter and pledge of the fullness and reality and continuity of the ministry of reconciliation: "Then said Jesus to them again, Peace be unto you: as my Father hath sent me . . . so send I you. And when he had said this, he breathed on them, and saith unto them, receive ye the Holy Ghost. Whose soever sins ye remit, they are remitted unto them; and whose soever sins ye retain, they are retained." If the Church of Jesus had not authority in His name and the sanctifying grace of the Holy Spirit to deal effectively and surely with human sin, how could sinful men, in the hour of their greatest need, be assured that their sins were indeed washed in the cleansing blood of the precious Lamb of God? We must always accept the reality of our pardon, and not look back upon the sinfulness of the past; we must move forward trustfully in the power of the Spirit, forgetting gladly those things which are behind and stretching forward unto those things which are before, pressing on toward the goal unto the prize of the high calling of God in Christ Jesus.

Sometimes the lesson of the daily-renewed penitence, which tradition so fitly ascribes to St. Peter, is lost upon us. We need to make an act of penitence carefully each day—something more than a conventional and cursory self-examination, which stirs no depths and brings no lasting healing. Our sins may be venial, not mortal—light, but not grave; but in any case they are sins, and they must be repented of and forgiven. Each night, as

The Spirit of Glory

we say our prayers, God offers us, in response to our sincere repentance, His assured pardon for the venial sins of the day. The Spirit of Glory is ready to repair the daily wear and tear, to put back what the sins of the day have rubbed thin or rubbed off, and to send us forth in the morning whole. It is our unforgiven negligences and ignorances that clog the wheels of our spiritual life—the little dust of sin unforgiven that gathers day by day, till it lies thick upon all the springs of our activity and robs us of the freshness of the day almost before morning comes. The Holy Spirit strives to achieve in us the glory of a penitent life.

[C]

It is the first work of love to assert holiness. God could not reveal Himself as love until He was known as holy. The burden of all the voices of revelation in the Old Testament is the same, "Holy, holy, holy, is the Lord of hosts." From the moment of the call of Abraham, Israel became the school of righteousness for the whole world. Its one mission was to declare the holiness of God. That is the heart of the message of Moses, and from the time when he had first proclaimed goodness as the supreme attribute of God, every fresh renewal in the life of the nation came from the assertion of the holiness of God. It is the same holiness which, in the teaching of the prophets compels and enforces the great judgments, that test all the people of the world. It was John the Baptist, the stern champion of righteousness, who was chosen to herald the coming of Love Incarnate.

Holiness

So the life that is linked with God Incarnate, by the indwelling of the Holy Ghost, must make goodness its first aim and the assertion of God's holiness the purpose of its vocation. The Church has no mission other than to proclaim God as the Holy One, to teach and set forward righteousness, and to make men holy by union with God. That is the only measure of its success. Its gospel is the good news of holiness. Its grace is the divine gift of holiness. Is that, however, the standard by which we judge our Churchmanship? How different would be the outlook today if we felt that all the mischances and evils of social life, all the discords and perplexities of industry and nations, all the moral failures and disappointments were just opportunities given to us by God for vindicating His holiness and establishing His righteousness!

A vision of the holiness of love gives life its purpose and binds us in the happy discipleship of Him who said, as He looked steadfastly at the sorrows and sins of men, "For their sakes I sanctify myself." It is in the sphere of holiness that the glory of the Spirit is revealed in human life.

A PRAYER FOR THE KNOWLEDGE OF JESUS

Blessed Spirit of God, breathe on us now and search for us the deep things of God, that guided by the light of thy wisdom we may enter into the mind of Christ, and being freed from all prejudice, ignorance, and sloth may be established in the truth of his holy gospel, who in the unity of the Father liveth and reigneth with thee, one God for ever and ever. Amen.

V

Sacrifice

THE heart of love is sacrifice, for sacrifice is the giving of self. In human experience there is always an element of pain in sacrifice, because, under the conditions of human imperfection and sin, there can be no perfect giving of self which does not involve suffering, but, thanks to freedom from sin, sacrifice is the radiant and joyful expression of perfect love. It is so in the Godhead.

[A]

Love in the being of God is the mutual self-giving in perfect harmony and bliss of the Father, the Son, and the Holy Ghost. That love is perfect sacrifice and utter happiness. It knows no limitations, and it is free from all restraints. When the love of God expresses itself in relation to created things, the elements of restraint and limitation appear and inject a note of suffering. So the love of the Father is construed in terms of sacrifice when He limits the immediate exercise of His own sovereign will and gives to man a will which is free to resist the divine purposes. It was the price which God was pleased to pay for human love—a price paid freely and without restraint, the only way it could be paid. Sacrifice on the

Sacrifice

part of God entered into the very conditions of creation. To that sacrifice man at first responded with an eager and joyful allegiance: his first obedience, in the early days of his undeveloped manhood, before his powers had matured, was a glad self-giving up to the limits of his being. He knew no pain of misdirected aim or thwarted love; his life was bright with the joy of innocence, and he was alert with the insight of the pure-hearted.

When the radiance of that first self-giving was clouded by sin, God sought a way of rescue by a new path of sacrifice: the sacrifice of redemption was added to the sacrifice of creation. So it is that the sacrifice of Jesus is revealed to us in two aspects. Jesus "being in the form of God, thought it not robbery to be equal with God: But made himself of no reputation, and took upon him the form of a servant, and was made in the likeness of men." The Son of God, infinite and eternal, subjected His divine self to the conditions of a human life—finite and earthly. The extent of that divine abasement is impossible for us to conceive. It is not merely that He who created all of creation came into creation itself, but the created was not as God had made it: Jesus came "in the likeness of sinful flesh, and for sin." The Sinless came to live in a world of sin. Thus the second aspect of His sacrifice is revealed—an even deeper condescension. "Being found in fashion as a man, he humbled himself, and became obedient unto death, even the death of the cross." It might have been deemed worthy of God, that having become man, He should experience manhood at its happiest, in the joy of unsullied splendor and in the glory of victorious achievement, but the way of the Redeemer

The Spirit of Glory

was the way of the Cross, and the Love of God was the way of sacrifice.

The Cross was not, however, the end of the divine resources of redemption: the Holy Spirit had yet to gather the fruit which the Cross of the Son should yield. The work of the Son would have been unfulfilled had not the Spirit brought men into the redeeming fellowship of Christ's Church. The third step, therefore, in the divine sacrifice was the self-giving of the Holy Spirit, a divine dwelling in the hearts of a stricken and sin-stained humanity, a constant guest, sadly grieved, often forgotten, but never despairing, an unfailing source of holiness, inspiration, and love. The Holy Spirit of Glory hides Himself in the hearts of men, resting upon us with His perpetual benediction, forming in us "the new man, which after God is created in righteousness and true holiness." If Jesus upon the Cross was able to make the perfect sacrifice—that supreme self-giving which availed to bring man to God—it was "through the eternal Spirit" that He "offered himself without spot to God." The Spirit of Glory and of Love is the Spirit of sacrifice in human life.

[B]

The Cross of Calvary is the symbol of perfect sacrifice—a sacrifice which manifests the perfect self-giving of a loving God. For the salvation of man God provided not a costly gift—not even a gift; instead He gave Himself. It was love's true giving of self. "God so loved the world, that he gave his only begotten Son." That is also the law of human love. The only human love which

Sacrifice

the writers of the New Testament mention is the love which is shed abroad in men's hearts by the Holy Spirit —a love that can never be satisfied with the gift of things. Whether it is our love for God or our love for one another, the law of love is the giving of self to the uttermost; no outward gift, however rich, suffices. There is no substitute for self; and if it is perfect love, it must be the whole self. Love cannot be satisfied with the self of yesterday; it must be the giving of the present self at its highest and best. How many married lives are wrecked just because husband and wife try to live on the sacrifices of the past, and not on the renewed giving of self in the richness of development and in the fullness of its present capacities! We must impart ourselves fully to one another, without reserve and with mutual reverence, and then the ideal of human love is attained and reciprocal self-giving makes us fully one.

It is impossible to give ourselves so as to lose our own independence or cease to be our best selves: we are still masters of ourselves; our originality, our individual personality cannot be dimmed nor destroyed by the self-giving of love; we remain ourselves, loosed from none of our responsibilities, but our personalities are gloriously enriched. In the same way God's love for man, with all its perfect giving of self, does not break the law of either divine or human personality, nor invade nor encroach upon the peculiar responsibilities of each. God's love gives us the Father's protecting care and sovereign rule, the Son's redeeming power, the Spirit's indwelling grace, but it does not make us God. Godlike we are meant to be, and love will make us so, but never will love make us

The Spirit of Glory

God. It is the part of the Spirit of Glory to achieve in us the perfected work of the love of God, and to build up our lives upon the pattern of the sinless love of the Incarnate Son. In His power our love for one another can reflect the glory of Jesus' own self-giving and be a mirror of the sacrifice that lies in the very heart of God.

The sacrifice of the love of Jesus is the sacrifice of the Good Shepherd—a pastoral love that does not wait for response, but persists through all indifference, neglect, ingratitude, and sin. Be it welcomed or rebuffed, the divine love continues its saving and protecting work, rescuing the wayward and the lost—strayed or lost through danger or death. The heart loves because it must love. "God commendeth his love toward us, in that, while we were yet sinners, Christ died for us." Such love, unsought and unrequieted, but never relaxed in its effort of sacrifice, is the supreme achievement of the human heart. Love begins in our childhood with naive trust in those about us: it is simple, passionless, unquestioning; but soon follows a love which looks eagerly for response and reciprocation—a love not satisfied, and sometimes not even stirred, unless there be a mutual and intimate affection in which one personality rests happily in another. Such is the love of normal friendship. Higher still, however, is the love which does not wait for reciprocation, which does not depend on response, but springs up instinctively, irresistibly, like the love of the mother for an infant child, or the love of the father for a faithless son. Such is the sacrificial love which the Holy Spirit seeks to create in the hearts of all those who are bound together in the fellowship of Christ's kingdom. Christ's work of love can

Sacrifice

be fulfilled only in Christ's spirit of love, and Christ's love is the sacrificial love—the love which gives of self and seeks no reward.

Only thus can we ourselves really love God. Quite apart from all that He has done for us and has given us, we must love Him for Himself. In the words of Catherine of Genoa "Not what proceedeth from Thee do I want, but Thee alone, O tender love." The one qualification which Jesus sought in those who would serve in His kingdom, was just this, "Simon, son of Jonas, lovest thou me?" Not practical capacity, not a sense of efficiency, not even joy in the work, but just unquestioning, unstinted, unspoiled love of Himself. Certainly for those who work for Jesus today, ministerial love is severely tested. Our service, be it ever so costly and ever so effectual, may go unwelcomed and unrewarded, may be received with resentment or indifference, its motives may be challenged and its worth belittled, but if it is motivated by that love which is the fruit of the Spirit's perfect work, it will not lose "the glory of going on;" it will be as unwearying as the eternal love of God Himself. By such service alone, Catherine of Siena used to say, could we in any worthy way make response to the love of Jesus. "Christ has loved us without being loved. We can only return that love at all in kind by loving those who love us not." That is the law of ministerial love—the law of sacrifice. God's workers need to remember it well. It is for that love and for that sacrifice, that the Spirit's gift of fortitude or "ghostly strength" is given us. So often, however, the continued apathy of irresponsiveness of those for whom and with whom we work dampens our hopefulness, dulls the fine

The Spirit of Glory

edge of our enthusiasm, and mars the perfection of our service. Yet, in the end, we know that sacrifice will triumph. The secret of love's victory is the secret of the Cross: Lacordaire revealed it to us in the words, "Those who are willing to die are the masters of those who want to live."

[C]

When we think of our self-giving in response to the love of God, we are brought to the high test of obedience. It is no secret that the acceptableness of the human life of Jesus in the Father's sight was His entire surrender of self in thought, word, and deed to the will of God—the complete obedience of life, the utter obedience unto death. The essence of the atoning power of our Lord's sacrifice is not to be found in its agony but in its obedience. The Holy Spirit, in whose power that obedience was won and kept, waits to achieve in us the glory of a like obedience.

Obedience is the measure of our love of God. St. Paul speaks of a "simplicity" which is "toward Christ." That is the secret of the obedient life—the secret of a life in which all the impulses and desires, all the instincts and passions, however contrary and rebellious, are guided by the Spirit towards one goal only—submission to God. The life is marked by a single-eyed devotion: there are no distractions, no rival aims, no hesitations, no divided motives. The Spirit guides the mind to know the will of God, inspires the heart to love it, and strengthens the will to obey it. Obedience means discipline, self-control,

Sacrifice

the mortification of many desires, a self-giving that is sacrificial. A life of obedience is not a sentimental repression of certain instincts in the interests of a morbid devotion, but an enrichment of the personality by a constant effort of Spirit-guided training, which brings all the faculties of life at their best and fullest to conformity to the will of Christ. The "simplicity" gained by the purification of desire and the harmony of conflicting motives leads the soul along the way of the Cross to its destined union with Christ. Strengthened with might by His spirit in the inner man, rooted and grounded in love, the soul comes to know the love of Christ and is filled with all the fullness of God.

If this be true—and it is true, we can realize the value of a rule of life, however simple, to guide us in our daily work. Nothing can be haphazard in our love of God, least of all the little disciplines with which we keep our faculties sensitive to His will. It is here that we need to rely upon the Holy Spirit. Nothing is too petty to submit to His inspiration. Each morning we should be able to offer a simple plan of the day for His acceptance and blessing. It is His blessing that gives dignity to the least effort that we make. He is indeed the Spirit of Glory, whose holy indwelling and consecrating power enable us to see God in what was mere earth before. We approach our work in the spirit of Pascal, when he said, "Let us resolve to do the little things as if they were the great things, because of the majesty of Jesus Christ who does them in us." The soul that submits itself to the sacrifice needed to make and to keep a "Rule of Life" preserves its God-given faculties from waste and fruitlessness, and builds up for itself a stable character and a habitual reliance upon God which will serve it in the hour of need. If the way of obedience seem too pedestrian and less spiritual and soaring than the way of vision, the experience of St. Teresa will reassure us: "The best things that I know came to me by obedience and not by revelation. . . . The love of God does not consist in being able to weep, not yet in delights and tenderness, but in serving with justice, fortitude, and humility. The other seems to me to receive rather than to give."

[D]

It is only when we realize that our love of God is a perpetual self-giving that we can understand the great part which the offering of the Eucharist plays in redeemed mankind's response to the love of God. We would give ourselves, we would give ourselves in perfection, we would offer glorious lives—a finished work of God, a sacrifice holy, harmless, undefiled, but no such sacrifice can we find in ourselves. Only God can find it, and only as we may be seen in Christ. We can offer Christ, who is the fullness of all we can hope to be, the pledge of our perfection, the summing up, the "recapitulation," as Irenaeus would call it, of all that is good in mankind. In our Lord's perfections we have a real share, with His righteousness we are truly identified, because He has become man, and we are in Him; through the gift of the Holy Spirit we have become very members incorporate in His mystical body, which is the blessed company of all faithful people.

Sacrifice

So the offering of obedience, which by ourselves we could not make, is made by the Church when we offer to God the Father upon our earthly altars the Eucharistic sacrifice of the sinless Christ and, through the merits of His perfect oblation, the offering of our own imperfect selves. That offering is not just a beautiful and expressive symbol of our true relation to God in Christ; is the actual lifting-up before the Father of that sacred Humanity, through whom we ourselves have access to God, and with whom our own manhood shines with the glory of eternal life.

If our love of God is shaped and formed in sacrifice, it is no wonder that our devotional life, our spiritual life—our life with God—to say nothing of our life with our fellow men, is often a life of sorrows. One might expect always to find sweetness and comfort in an intimate relationship with God, but the experience of the saints teaches us otherwise. Of all the great saints, whose inner life of prayer has been revealed to us, few have not passed through the fiery trial of prolonged gloom and weary desolation, and learned to say, with Mark Rutherford, "I love Christ's glooms better than the world's worm-eaten joys." It is a hard lesson in sacrifice, but one which we, most ordinary and most simple lovers of God, must learn.

We must never be surprised, or think ourselves bereft of God, or wanting in reality and earnestness, if we find difficulties in our prayers and a bareness in our communions. "This is the way," says Bossuet, "that Christ deals with us—His ordinary method. He draws souls to Himself, He gives them a hunger that cannot be satisfied, He wins them, masters them, binds them. He holds

The Spirit of Glory

them so intimately that they have no life apart from Him, and when they are chained and all escape is impossible, He withdraws Himself, He vanishes and tests them by the most dreadful desolation." Such is the sacrifice which marks the self-giving of love in our devotional life. To be really lost in God is to be forgetful of self, so that the heart has no place save for Him alone, that it is so intent on God's perfection that there is no feeling of own desolation. For us who cannot thus be lost in God, it is sufficient to remember that the longing of a loving heart for God, and its endurance of unwelcome difficulties for His sake, is one of the most perfect prayers. Remember, the Spirit "helpeth our infirmities" and achieves in us the glory of steadfast union with God.

[E]

To recognize sacrifice as a vital element in our love for one another is much easier than to see it in our love for God. The love for one another, which can be steadfast and enduring through all the sacrifices which love demands, can only be a love which is born of the Spirit. The Spirit gives us the vision of other souls which God Himself has. He searches the deep things of God, and in the light of that vision love is strengthened for sacrifice. For like Lacordaire, after his conversion, we see the world with new eyes: it assumes nobler proportions as we do ourselves; we see in it a noble sufferer needing help, and we can imagine no happiness greater than that of ministering to it under the eye of God with the devotion of all our powers. The proof of the reality of the Spirit's

Sacrifice

effectual indwelling in our hearts is not merely tranquility and peace, not any emotional satisfaction, nor rapturous ecstasy, but sacrificing service.

It is an interesting and intriguing study to observe in the works of the great painters the economy and skill with which they use their brightest colors. In a landscape where the prevailing hues are grey and green there will be a little touch of bright red—the shawl of a woman crossing the field, a sailor's cap, a child's stocking, the shutter of a house; yet blot out for a moment that touch of red, cover it with your finger, hide it from sight, and the picture has lost its beauty—gone is all the distinction, and the tone has become dull and flat. It is the touch of red that serves to bring out the glory of the whole composition and give value to all the other colors in the scene. In human life each tiny act of sacrifice, red with the hue of Calvary, reveals beauty in the dull drab colors of the world and throws a glory over the simplest scenes. The glory is the glory of God; it comes from God; it reveals God; it springs up in the service of God. Sacrifice is not all pain; it brings its own happiness. There was joy set before Him even in those very moments of agony when Jesus endured the Cross, despising its shame.

"You must fix your eye and heart unflinchingly on Christ and His reproach," said Dr. Benson as he took farewell of his Sixth Form at Wellington College. "You must adore it, you must achieve it. For there is no treasure like the reproach of Christ, understood and loved and lived." No headmaster has ever started his pupils on their career of service with words of nobler inspiration or more profound spiritual insight. The Spirit's gift of joy is never

The Spirit of Glory

more steadfast, never more compelling, never more eager, than when it is rooted in sacrifice. Even in our own narrow experience of sacrifice we can realize the truth of the well-known words of Thomas à Kempis, "In the Cross is protection from enemies, in the Cross is infusion of heavenly sweetness. In the Cross is strength of mind, in the Cross is joy of spirit." The eternal Spirit through whom Christ offered Himself without spot to God, will enable us in our self-offering and sacrifice to reflect, as in a mirror, the glory of the Lord, and to be transformed by His glory into the image itself.

A PRAYER FOR OBEDIENCE

Eternal and blessed Spirit of God, grant to me day by day such trust in the fullness of thy indwelling, that I may ever commit myself to thy love. Keep me steadfast in temptation, triumphant over sin, and zealous for thy glory. Make me responsive to thy will and obedient to thy calling, alike in sorrow and in joy, that I may follow faithfully in the steps of him who has died upon the Cross for me, that I might live unto God, even Jesus Christ our Lord. Amen.

VI

Sympathy

THE most fruitful and creative element in love is sympathy. Sympathy is the sincerity of a loving fellowship which makes us live in the life of another. To create that sympathy between man and God is the aim of the Holy Spirit's indwelling. The sympathy of Jesus is the fruit of the Incarnation and the secret of the Atonement. So in the Incarnation Jesus was "in all things made like unto his brethren," He was "touched with the feeling of our infirmities," He was "in all points tempted like as we are"—His fellow-feeling with us was complete. He knew human nature not only as God, but also as Man. The full extent of that sympathy was manifested on the Cross. When all legal and forensic images fail to explain the mystery of the atoning power of the death of Jesus, we come back to the sympathy, which marks all human love, and find in it an experience which takes us to the heart of the Atonement. We must not think that the price at which Christ bought us was merely His life-blood, or only the obedience in death; rather it was the unbroken obedience of all the thirty-three years of His earthly life. Death was the climax, the last test of that obedience; it was not the whole price, but the last, the largest installment. It was a whole life of perfect sympathy which Christ offered.

The Spirit of Glory

When all metaphors and analogies have been used and all the ideas of purchase, ransom, and penalty have been exhausted in vain, it is in the sympathy of love itself, that familiar human experience common to all true lovers, that we find the leading clue to the mystery of the Atonement. It was because Jesus took our human nature so fully to Himself, because He ranged Himself so completely with us in the vicissitudes of human life, because He identified Himself so truly with our experience, that He could actually live in our lives. "Him, who knew no sin" God could make "to be sin, that we might be made the righteousness of God in him." He who atoned for the sin of all men is the perfect embodiment of perfect sympathy—a sympathy which is not a mere feeling of fellowship, but an act of identifying and everlasting and glorious union.

[A]

Human love is made perfect in sympathy. At the first outset of love there are ecstasies and raptures and thrilling impulses of wonder and affection, but that is not the fullness of love. The profoundest love is that which has been admitted to the intimate sharing of joys and fears, which has lasted and proved true after the testing of many a sacrifice, a love which in its ripe maturity is forbearing, uplifting, unifying—not the first transport of ecstatic passion, but the stable, serene, and tranquil habit of mutual affection, with its sure insight, its sensitive comprehension, its gentle patience, its linking of two lives in one. That is the crown of love, where one lives in the life of the other. Such love is the love of Jesus: the love that

Sympathy

reads the heart of Mary Magdalene, that bears gently with the secrecy of Nicodemus, that understands the contradictions of St. Peter, that interprets the unspoken loyalty of the thief upon the cross. That is the love to which the heart of the beloved disciple St. John made response, the love which upheld him through his long ministry and enabled him to leave to the Church that picture of incarnate love which has never ceased to be the inspiration of the Christian life. That was what he taught when in his later years he repeated with a reiteration which became irksome to the younger generation, "Little children, love one another. It is the commandment of the Lord, and if it alone be done, it is enough." That is a matter which we ourselves must consider carefully and honestly: Can we do it well enough to say that it is enough?

First, there is our sympathy with God. Just as in human love, our love for God has its first ecstasies. There is a "first love" which carries us along in a fine rapture with a fire and beauty all its own. Love is something deeper than rapture: it means the sharing of ideals, the understanding of God's purpose, the adoration of His holiness, the vision of His majesty, the acceptance of His will. It was exactly in this manner that as Man Jesus showed His love of the Father, and it was exactly that spot in the armor of the Perfect Man that Satan hoped to pierce. The point of all the temptations lay just in this, that they sought to sever the sympathy of man with God. Would Jesus hold fast by the ideals of God? Would He be true to God's vision of man's life? Could He be found disloyal to the method and purpose of God's kingdom? Jesus as perfect Man, in whom the Holy Spirit of glory recreated

The Spirit of Glory

the lost image of God, held His will truly steadfast to the divine ideal. Such is the loyalty of love.

What Jesus sought for in vain among His followers, and more especially among the Apostles, was the sympathy of a love which could enter into the spiritual grandeur of His mission. The Galileans were ready to accept His leadership for the attainment of their own hopes of national victory, and the Apostles were ready to rejoice in His fellowship and to find inspiration in His teaching and take pleasure in serving Him, who was Himself among them "as one that serveth;" but a heart that savored the things of God, Jesus could not find. That was the secret of the Apostles' failure. Jesus, however, knew that only the coming of the Holy Spirit was needed to create the sympathy that was lacking. With His insight into the realities of their hearts Jesus could commit the Apostles confidently to His Father, even on the very night of their desertion, in words which sound to us almost unbelievable. "They have kept thy word. Now they have known that all things whatsoever thou has given me are of thee. For I have given unto them the words which thou gavest me; and they have received them, and have known surely that I came out from thee, and they have believed that thou didst send me."

Jesus knew that it would be the work of the Holy Spirit soon to complete in them the glory of perfect love by guiding them into all truth in "the mind of Christ." His long prayer ends with the words "O righteous Father, the world hath not known thee: but I have known thee, and these have known that thou hast sent me. And I have declared unto them thy name, and will declare it:

Sympathy

that the love wherewith thou hast loved me may be in them, and I in them." Jesus had already begun to make the Father known to the disciples. The way in which He yet will make the Father known would be through the teaching of the Holy Ghost. It would be through the Spirit's indwelling that the love, wherewith the Father loved the Son, would be in them—that love which was eternal sympathy and mutual harmony of will. It was not merely the very love of God, the blissful concord of heart and mind and will, which was to be theirs: Jesus Himself would be theirs through the gift of the Spirit: He would bring divine love to abide with them forever: He would be in them, and they in Him.

[B]

That sympathy of love which Jesus could not find in His Apostles during the days of His earthly mission is ours to offer Him now in the power of the Spirit. It is the secret of our life of prayer. Prayer is the union of our will with the will of God; it is the constant effort of the soul that loves God; it is a lesson never fully learned in this world; and the Holy Spirit is the teacher. "The Spirit also helpeth our infirmities: for we know not what we should pray for as we ought: but the Spirit . . . maketh intercession for us with groanings which cannot be uttered. And he that searcheth the hearts knoweth what is the mind of the Spirit, because He maketh intercession for the saints according to the will of God." It is "the mind of the Spirit" that leads us to pray according to the will of God.

The Spirit of Glory

The first lesson in prayer which the Spirit has to do with vision of God: it is the knowledge of God that is the measure of our prayer. Here we often find our first failure in prayer. We do not seek the inspiration of the Holy Ghost to reveal to us the glory of God. "Ye ask, and receive not, because ye ask amiss." We ask amiss because we see only ourselves and our needs, and have no vision of the glory of God. We see not His purposes, we have no sympathy with His holiness, no understanding of His will.

It is the Holy Spirit who schools us in prayer: "the Spirit searcheth all things, yea, the deep things of God." The good things which God has prepared for them that love Him, we cannot know by ourselves. "God hath revealed them unto us by his Spirit. . . . The things of God knoweth no man, but the Spirit of God. Now we have received, not the spirit of the world, but the spirit which is of God; that we might know the things that are freely given to us by God." Thus the knowledge both of God Himself and of His purposed gifts to man is the work of the Holy Spirit; we must therefore attempt to increase that knowledge, in the power of the Spirit, before we come to the consideration of our own needs. Francis de Sales says of the devout soul, "It is enough for the soul that loves, that He whom it loves more than itself is heaped with blessings."

The world of spiritual realities is greatly unknown to us because we have not put enough trust in the guidance of the Holy Spirit. The side of the life of prayer, which is spoken of as the prayer of contemplation or the prayer of faith, which we sometimes think beyond our powers,

Sympathy

is well within our reach, if only we will let the Holy Spirit direct our devotion. The quiet work of the Holy Spirit takes the place of our difficult reasoning and allows us to wait upon the grace of His inspiration. He alone can really draw the soul to prayer; we do not come of ourselves; and where He draws, He guides. So He brings us into the presence of God in the spirit of love. "The progress of the soul in perfection," says St. Teresa, "does not consist in thinking much but in loving much." It is the love of God engendered by the Spirit that leads us onward in the knowledge of God—the fruit of prayer. The Spirit directs us first to be joyful in the grandeur of God. We see Him raised infinitely beyond the creaturely life of the universe, and our hearts are stirred to praise and worship. Then the Spirit reveals the goodness and loveableness of God, and we rest in His beauty and adore His holiness. Then the Spirit guides us to the good purposes of God, and we bow before His sovereign will and offer ourselves to fulfill our part in the accomplishment of His kingdom. That is the way by which the Spirit quickens in us a desire for God. That is the first step in prayer—the creation of a real sympathy with God. Sympathy, it will be seen, is not a stirring of the emotions, it is not an affection of the senses; it is rather a directing of the will to accept the loving purpose of God. Thus the Spirit leads us to see God and to find in Him a love worthy of all our devotion, a wisdom which is life's inspiration, and a will which it is our glory to obey.

The second lesson in prayer which the Holy Spirit gives is the vision of ourselves as God sees us. When we have seen God, we can see ourselves; and the first thing we

The Spirit of Glory

see is our worth to God: we are worth more in God's sight than we are in our own, we are fellow-workers with God, and God has a use for us. Our act of prayer and fellowship helps us to fulfill God's purposes for us. We have no illusions about the limitations of our finite nature, but we realize how the dignity and capacity of that nature are enriched for us by the indwelling of the Holy Ghost: a new self-respect heightens our sense of responsibility and rouses in us new ideals. While we make oblation of ourselves to God, it is right, it is needful, that we should recognize the worth of that offering: in God's eyes it has value.

On the one hand, the vision of ourselves as God sees us lays open the depths of our shame and leads us to a due humility in the presence of God. We are conscious that we have no merits of our own to plead, we know that we can stand before God only through the merits of the sinless Redeemer, and so we must always approach God as penitents. That places us at once in the right relation to God as suppliants. We confess the undeserved bounty of God's generosity, and we know there is no limit to His grace, therefore we need never be restrained in our hopes of succor. A sense of thankfulness, so often absent in the life of prayer, can never fail to stimulate us to an unselfish recognition of the wonder of God's goodness to us and to a fuller understanding of that "giveness," which is the peculiar mark of the Christian life. It is not merely that we are ready to magnify the sovereignty of Almighty God and to surrender ourselves as willing instruments of God's divine purpose, but that we are thrilled and captivated by the sublime grandeur of the

Sympathy

grace of God which fills our undeserving lives with heavenly power, enriches us with a treasury of opportunity, and sustains us with constant spiritual strength. For us, as we pray, life is always opening new doors to new visions.

> What's life to me?
> Where'er I look is fire, where'er I listen,
> Music—and where I tend, bliss evermore.

On the other hand, while we are conscious of our weakness, we are also conscious of our privilege and dignity as fellow-workers with God, called by Him to take an appointed part in the work of divine redemption. It is the Holy Spirit who assures us of the rights of sonship, who marks out our individual sphere of service, and who divides the gift of God to us severally as He wills. It is as Spirit-born and Spirit-bearing sons of God that we fulfill our part in the Incarnation. Jesus has redeemed man's natural powers from the grave misuse to which disobedience had committed them, but the Holy Spirit makes them apt and serviceable instruments of God's saving will, and by the inspiration of the same Spirit, we are guided to a true sense of vocation and directed along God's chosen path of service. Drawn therefore by the Spirit of Glory, we come with confidence and without scruple to our work of prayer, knowing that it is the very activity in the sphere of God's kingdom to which the King has called us. It is a work, not of supererogation, but of necessity, and its motive is not our own spiritual satisfaction, but God's needs. We seek not comfort, but the world's salvation. Understanding the thirst of God

The Spirit of Glory

for the souls of men, we pray in the spirit of sympathy. It is thus that all our trials and discomforts and desolations in prayer are lost in the glad sense of thankfulness to God for allowing us in the power of the Holy Spirit to take our part in that sinless and availing advocacy of Jesus which is the world's redemption.

The last lesson in prayer is given to us by the Spirit of Glory when He reveals to us the lives of others as they are in the sight of God. If God has taught us what we ourselves are in His sight, we know with what sympathy and love we must look upon the lives of those for whom we pray. Intercession becomes dull and loses its attraction as soon as the light of sympathy dies out of our hearts. It is just the vision of God that we need: we must ask for His boundless sympathy, His tender charity, His generous estimate, His pardoning look. We must realize what those souls are to Him, imagine what He wants them to be, what He sees them becoming. We must realize what He gives them to do, how He trusts them to serve. When you pray for others, see them, if you can, as God sees them, that is, not alone, but in their surroundings. Encourage yourself to visualize the actual conditions of their life; picture the home, the workshop, the office, the school, and search out the difficulties of their work and their daily experience. Your intercession is to help in strengthening them, to increase the good in them. Your prayers are to enable what God alone can see in them to become realized in their lives.

It was said of Michelangelo that when a friend found him rough-hewing a shapeless block of marble in his

Sympathy

workshop and asked him what he was doing, he replied, "I am letting the angel out." The artist's eyes saw hidden in the massive block the delicate beauty of those angelic figures with which he was to adorn the facade of an Italian cathedral church. He saw them, and he could release them, but they were hidden to other eyes. So in our intercession the sympathizing love of the Spirit trains us in the vision of God, and our prayer becomes confident, constant, and availing, because it is marked by the insight of God. Thus we can understand something of the work of the Spirit of Glory in training us in the ways of prayer. Bossuet in his own life of prayer experienced the same thing. He realized the comfort of the Holy Spirit's continual support—"The soul leaves reasoning behind and is content with a happy contemplation which holds it peaceful and attentive, ready to receive the divine operation and impression given it by the Holy Spirit. It does little and receives much. Its work is happy, yet most productive. And as it draws nearer and nearer to the source of every light of grace and virtue, these gifts are bestowed upon it with yet greater abundance." It is through the gift of the Spirit that we gain the sympathy of Christ which is the inspiration of all our prayer. When we plead the merits of Jesus, we can approach the throne of grace in the very spirit of Jesus Himself, with the sympathy of a love which is eternal and infinite.

A PRAYER FOR LOVE

O Holy Ghost, by whom the love of God is shed abroad in our hearts; Kindle in us the flame of thy love, that

The Spirit of Glory

stirred by the fire of thy indwelling we may set our affection on things above, and taught by thy inspiration may show our love for Jesus in service to those for whom he died; who with thee and the eternal Father liveth and reigneth, God for ever and ever. Amen.

VII

Comfort

HOWEVER the title "Paraclete" is translated—Consoler (for the loss of Christ), Advocate, or Comforter, it is the part of the Holy Spirit's office to bring consolation as well as strength to meet the needs of suffering humanity. Few needs are more evident today in the religious world than the need of true and assured strength in spiritual things. Even those who have professed and called themselves Christians for many years will be found declaring that they find no great strength in their faith or even the practice of their religion. The Christian life is for them a dull, joyless routine, with little sunshine and no constant gladness. Beyond the fold of Christian living is a pitiable lack of genuine cheerfulness and no sense of certitude or abiding happiness. A listless apathy, a pessimistic resignation, a critical and perpetual discontent, an artificial gaity that deceives no one, a concern with "busy-ness"— all are kill-joys of life.

Instead of seeking out, or depending on, or tolerating kill-joys, people should search for and open themselves, their hearts and minds and souls, to the Holy Ghost, for joy—real joy—is one of the universal gifts of the Spirit's indwelling. Joy is the reflection in our lives of one of the perfections of God. The life in God is marked by a radiant and eternal joy called blessedness. What is blessedness in God is happiness in man. The power of perfect joy and contentment in all that God is and all that He does belongs to God; man's true joy lies in that which gives pleasure to God. The Holy Spirit teaches us what are the objects in which God takes pleasure, and enables us to hold them persistently before us as our steadfast ideals and to take abiding joy in them. That God dwells in the heart of man is not only an indication of divine joy, it is also a reflection of divine hope. By looking at life with the happy vision of God, we too are joyful through hope. "The greatest sign of the divine grace dwelling in the soul is joy," said an old saint. The inspiring motto, "Serve God and be cheerful," suggests the true source of all joy. The spirit of happiness, the sense of comfort, consciousness of blithe freedom from restraint, active, bubbling, buoyant gladness—these are the marks of every true follower of Christ. Spiritual happiness is not the strange and exclusive privilege of super-eminent saints, but the prized heritage of every Christian. The habit of joy is a marked feature of the mystery of the indwelling Christ. It may very well be that in the case of exalted natures, Christian joy shows itself in extravagances of happy rapture. When we see St. Francis of Assisi reviving the religious life of medieval Christendom with the bright and radiant spirit of Christian liberty, when we read his joyous "Canticle of the Sun," and hear his ecstatic paean of praise breaking forth in the repeated cry "My God and All," we are aware of a uniquely capacious nature. We are ready to believe that St. Francis was capable of greater love and moved to greater joy than we

Comfort

can experience; yet joy in Christ is for us all, "through the touching of the Holy Spirit"—an everyday gift, a common blessing, a promised endowment which all can claim.

The joy is in Christ Himself. Jesus speaks of it as "my joy" which "no man taketh from you." It is not only a gift of God, but it is a gift which centers in God Himself. That is why so many miss its happiness. It does not center around self. Its only satisfaction is in God. It is for those whose life is ruled by the certainty that Jesus is God, who realize that in the fullness of His Incarnation He has forever taken human life up into Himself and has filled it with the blessedness of God. If anyone doubted the truth of His promise, the very lives of the Apostles would provide ample proof of the reality of the new and unconquerable power of the gladness with which Christ has enriched life. After the gift of the Spirit at Pentecost the Apostles revealed an intense and vibrant happiness, an enthusiastic confidence, a zealous assurance, which girded them for heroic tasks and carried them triumphantly through persecution and through death. Nothing could quench it, nothing could beat it down. They carried in their hearts a new music, the melody of the everlasting chime, which no earthly terror could silence nor disturb. Such joy is not a sudden flash in a dark night of gloom and sorrow: it is the upbreaking of the perpetual goodness and gaity of God. As St. Augustine says, "No man can hide from Thy sunshine." So joy in Christ brings to us our portion of devout and thankful gladness, spreading through all the avenues of life—not a momentary rapture, not a sudden inspiration,

The Spirit of Glory

but a habit, an abiding attitude of the soul, the herald of eternal bliss.

Joy in Christ, which the Spirit of Glory ministers, is a gladness that is safe from every assault of man or evil spirit: it cannot be tainted nor touched nor taken away. The acceptance of Christ as Saviour brings with it a happiness which is invulnerable, a joy undarkened by any cloud of sorrow or of pain. There are—there must be—realms of life and reaches of experience in which we can seriously trouble one another's happiness (the world would be indeed a world of chartered selfishness if it were not so!), for the nearer we are to each other in sympathy and affection, the greater is the pain which we have the power to inflict. We can fill other lives with sunshine, or we can cloud them with gloom, but only up to a certain point: there is a deep seat of eternal and abiding happiness, which is beyond the reach of trouble or molesting care, beyond the touch of man, and that is where the Spirit of God is enthroned. Men may trouble our lives however they will with hostility, pain, and malice, but there is an interior sphere of calm and peace, an inner shrine of joy and happiness, a secret fellowship with Christ, which remains beyond their reach. Just as in the great ocean the winds may lash the waves to foam and fury while the hidden depths lie immovable, so our outward lives may make quick and sensitive response to the varying winds of human intercourse which blow across the sea of life, but the soul in its profoundest depths may keep a quiet sanctuary of serene, untroubled calm. That is where God touches life; that is where we are secured to the tender love of Jesus. His strength and

Comfort

love enwrap us, steady us, establish us in peace, and reveal to us new ways of fellowship and fill us with the calm restfulness and bliss of God.

[B]

The secret of divine comfort lies in the moral assurance of salvation which the acceptance of the grace of the indwelling Spirit gives. The soul that is linked with God in sacramental fellowship has that certain unction from the Holy One. Speaking from experience in the midst of persecution and hardship, St. John could cry out, "We know . . . we know!" That assurance and that conviction is the secret of Christian happiness. Sin alone can disturb that knowledge and mar that happiness. However small the actual achievement may be for the soul that is making a sincere, earnest, and conscious effort, there is always comfort and gladness. We have no right to doubt God's leading, no right to distrust the adequacy of His revelation nor the sufficiency of His grace. He has given us the Spirit to help our infirmities. He sustains us in our effort of perseverance; and however little we may seem at first to succeed, the very effort itself must be a ground of happiness and an assurance of the divine approval.

Some sense of God's approval is needed for our constant endurance. St. Teresa said that it was impossible for anyone to have courage for great undertakings who did not perceive that he was favored by God. It has been said that "man has to think greatly of himself when he pursues his own task against all opposition." We can do so only when we are joyfully assured of the covenanted

The Spirit of Glory

assistance of God and are happy in the knowledge of His confidence and trust in us.

The life of St. Francis of Assisi with its wonderful experience of happiness reveals the need of spiritual joy as an incentive to effort. There was a moment in his work when great doubt beset him. The new fraternity was just beginning to develop: it was still small, still in its first experimental stage, when he was confronted with the sins of the past, and all the vision of the future was blocked out. In agonizing prayer he cast himself upon God, imploring mercy for his sins, when suddenly there came to him the complete and indubitable assurance of divine forgiveness and the power to persevere to the end, and, as in a dream, he saw the little company of the brotherhood of poverty growing into a large and effective army of Christ. From that vision of victory he rose a changed man; from that moment his purpose never faltered, his faith never failed. In the very face of God he had found peace. Now he could sing unceasingly the praise of the Lord most high, now he could conquer as a faithful soldier and servant of God.

In the same spirit Madame Chantal used to confess that the secret of her happiness and steadfast endurance through all the long terrors of spiritual temptation, was the personal assurance of divine fellowship which God had given her through the indwelling of the Holy Spirit. Someone said to her once that, in her own experience, she had been compelled to be content with knowing just that God was God, never daring to call Him *her* God. Madame Chantal replied that for herself, however tormented and beaten down her life had been, it had never been so

Comfort

low that she could not say, "O God, Thou art my God and the good of my heart," for while the Faith had taught her that He was God, the baptism which she had received made her realize that of a truth He was *her* God. That is the true ground of comfort in God, that is the security of the sacramental fellowship which the Holy Spirit inaugurates and cherishes and develops, that is the true gift of God to His children. "The Spirit itself beareth witness with our spirit, that we are children of God: And if children, then heirs . . . of God, and joint-heirs with Christ."

The Holy Paraclete has other gifts: He adds to our divine fellowship with God a sense of sweetness and consolation—something not reserved for special or contemplative souls, but something shared in some degree with all who know Christ. God gives us a sensible joy in our religious life, a comfort which is assured to those who are seeking to do His blessed will. It is revealed in a quiet sense of divine approval, and a feeling of spiritual sweetness, which casts over life a certain serenity and peace, and which creates in our souls an atmosphere of restful assurance that all difficulties can be met and overcome. It brings a simple joy in Christ Himself, and a simple delight in His Will. The happiness which it brings is not a mere selfish sense of personal comfort and consolation, but an active consciousness of divine approval, a pure delight in the majesty and goodness of God, and a single-hearted joy in the fulfillment of His Will.

The feeling of divine comfort can be accompanied by temptations, real or imaginary; the truth is told by the fruits, and the test never fails. Divine comfort is no

The Spirit of Glory

morbid imagination, no neurotic fancy, if it leads to effective issues in the life. It does not end in mere sensuous feeling, but gives a new vision of God and inspires new obedience; it gives a new steadfastness in the face of temptation, a new courage in the face of difficulties; it makes us gentle and tender towards others, unselfish and gracious in our ministries of love; it keeps our thoughts in the way of holiness and makes us more scrupulous in our use of sacramental grace. It is thus no deceitful form of spiritual selfishness, no enervating luxury of the religious life, but a genuine strength which reaches out through us to others. Very often a sense of spiritual comfort is given to us as beginners, not as a mere bait or lure, but as a needed help, to do a real work in our hearts, to enable us to drive our way through the new difficulties which beset our first steps along the way of holiness, to disperse the gloom which darkens the earliest efforts of our devotion, to strengthen us for heroic service. It is for this that the Spirit of the Lord leads us out of the depths, it is for this that He feeds us in green pastures, and leads us beside the waters of comfort.

[C]

The way of divine comfort is not the only way of the Spirit, for there is also the way of consolation. God may sometimes however withhold the sense of consolation. St. John of the Cross says there are two ways up the great hill of spiritual attainment. One is directly upwards, steep and difficult, straight and narrow, the way of pure faith

Comfort

and devoid of spiritual consolation; the second way twists in tortuous spirals round the mount, and is slow: it includes knowledge, counsel, sweetness, assurance, and glory —the way of the mystic. Perhaps most of us use both paths at different times in our ascent, but for the most part we confine ourselves to the more gentle ascent of the path of divine sweetness and consolation. Now and then God offers the steeper path without comfort until we meet again on a higher level and the easier path from which for a while we were called.

There are indeed times when the added sense of spiritual consolation, which reinforces and enlivens the assurance we have in Christ Jesus, may be withdrawn or withheld. We can understand why it may be good for us sometimes to miss it: it may be withdrawn in order to teach us that it is the gift of God, and not due to our own effort, not the reward of our own deserts. "My peace I give unto you." We may be inclined to think of it as a part of our natural equipment, or to rest in it as an end in itself and not as a call to a fresh realization of God, for it is easy, very easy indeed, to be satisfied with our own happy feelings, and fail to make a new effort of obedience and service for which God's gifts are meant to prepare us.

Sometimes we may well believe that our Lord loves to see us laboring on without the help of favors, because then He sees in us a likeness of His own ever-blessed suffering. It may be that in the mysterious providences of the Holy Spirit's working, God has something to achieve in us which can be fulfilled only in the moments of coldness and lack of conscious favor. As in medical practice today

The Spirit of Glory

the physician will sometimes cause the body to be absolutely insensibile and unconscious, in order that the arms or legs may be entirely relaxed and wholly responsive to his will; so we can conceive that the Heavenly Physician may for a while induce in us a spiritual anaesthesia, that in His own secret way He may heal our souls, and in the hidden depths of our subconscious life attune our wills to an entire obedience. At least, when those moments of numbness and spiritual insensibility come, we shall know that it is not because God is far away, but rather because He is near. An experience of coldness and gloom will suggest the need of a simple act of penitence, so that we may be purged from all the sin and selfishness that hinder the way of God's will in us. If the consolation of the Spirit be still withheld, we shall know that God has deemed us worthy of the more difficult way and is calling us, even through the trial of desolation, nearer to Himself. Be there desolation or comfort, we shall always learn to take joy in God just because He is God. Always there is that source of comfort ministered to us by the Spirit of Glory, if only faith be strong enough to hold fast the vision of God, which in brighter moments has been so abundantly made sure to us. It is in the power of the Spirit of Glory that we learn to fashion

> A life that stands, as all true lives have stood,
> Firm rooted in the faith that God is good.

A PRAYER FOR GLADNESS

Holy and blessed Spirit, eternal font of happiness and joy; Comfort us when, amid the sorrows and cares of life,

Comfort

we are cast down and faint of heart, and grant that being renewed by thy gracious inspiration we may go on our way rejoicing, and at length appear triumphant before the Father of our joy and gladness; through Jesus Christ our Lord. Amen.

VIII

Sacrament

THE vagueness with which every language expresses the word Spirit creates a certain amount of haziness of thought about the Holy Ghost. That vagueness is intensified by the difficulty of understanding the personality of One to whom the title Spirit is given. For the First and Second Persons of the Blessed Trinity we have human analogies of fatherhood and sonship, which help us to understand something about their personality. The terms are inadequate to the co-eternal Father-Son relationship, for no human words in which eternal truths are clad can ever convey to us more than a shadow of the realities for which they stand. The titles do however safeguard effectively the fact that They are Persons and act towards us in a personal way, but we do not have in human life a relationship which can fully explain the Holy Spirit's relationship in the Blessed Trinity. In the absence of any human analogy men readily think of the Holy Ghost as an energy, a power, or an attribute of God rather than as Himself God. Their difficulty in apprehending the personality of the Holy Spirit affects their understanding of the methods by which He works in human life. The Holy Spirit is not a vague, indeterminate, hidden influence working capriciously and sporadically—a way which no

Sacrament

one can calculate or foresee; He is, rather, One with the Father and the Son, not only in the fullness and distinctiveness of His Person, but also in the methodical and constant ways of His dealing with man.

The way of God's dealing with man is fully disclosed to us in the Incarnation. The Incarnation is not the will of one Person alone in the Godhead, but the will and the work of Father, Son, and Spirit—one God fulfilling one purpose. The principle of the Incarnation reveals the way in which the Holy Spirit is pleased to act towards us—the minister of an Incarnate Lord, sent from the glory of the Resurrection and Ascension to carry on and fulfill the work in our time and place which Jesus already had begun at another time, another place. It is along definite lines of outward and visible mediation, which we call sacramental, that the Holy Spirit must be expected to work. The reality of the Incarnation and the certainty of the Resurrection guarantee to us a like certainty and reality—and effectiveness of the Holy Spirit in His purpose to establish and sustain our fellowship with God. For new and glorious ends of human intercourse with God, the Spirit of Glory uses creaturely elements, visible means, outward activities, all of which are simple and natural, and common to all of us.

[A]

"The Spirit of God moved upon the face of the waters." The Spirit of Glory first showed Himself in creation as the Giver of Life. All life remains a constant witness to the unceasing activity of the immanent Spirit of God.

The Spirit of Glory

The world is something more than mere creation by a wise and omnipotent God; it is something more because the ever-active Spirit of Glory is constantly shaping, moulding, inspiring, strengthening and ordering all things graciously. In every order of creation, it is the Spirit of Glory who leads each separate life to the fulfillment of its true purpose in the great scheme of the universe. Man, ordained to be that universe's crown and glory, is alone conscious of the God-given powers by which he is raised above all other creatures. Man knows himself to be compact of body and of soul, and that each is needed for the fullness of his life and personality. In the instinctive actions of daily life he recognizes how surely the soul needs the body as the organ of its self-expression. The gladness of the heart reveals itself with simple naturalness in dance and song: the smiling face, the furrowed brow, the hesitating gait, the uplifted eye—all are the outward, corporal, sacramental expression of the moods of the soul.

In the intimate fellowship of soul and body, man knows that the soul claims the mastery. The body has its own impulses and instincts, which may war against the soul: it is man's life work, with discipline and ceaseless effort, to ensure the sovereignty of the soul; it is also the constant enterprise of the Holy Spirit. His indwelling accepted, welcomed, and encouraged, hallows our natural instincts, harmonizes the warring and contrary impulses of the soul, calms the clamoring strife of the passions, and brings peace, so that the body realizes its true dignity as the temple of the Holy Ghost.

When man approaches God in the moments of his highest earthly worship, he does not divest himself of

Sacrament

his body, but offers it consciously as the obedient instrument of the soul; all his powers and senses take their part in enriching the oblation of his whole manhood. Indeed there may come a time when our bodies have been so well trained to cooperate with the soul, and the soul has been roused to so great an ecstasy, that the body seems to lose all senses. In moments of danger the body has been known to perform phenomenal feats of strength; in moments of divine contemplation the body can lose itself so completely that only the soul's communication with God remains. Such a rapture St. Augustine experienced as he gazed with St. Monica from the open window at Ostia. Thinking of the eternal life of the saints, he soared Godwards with glowing heart and mind: "If the tumult of the flesh were hushed, hushed these shadows of earth, sea, sky, hushed the heavens and the soul itself, so that it should pass beyond itself, if all dreams were hushed, and all revelations of sense and every tongue and every symbol, if all that comes and goes were hushed, suppose we heard Him with no intermediary at all." With one thought's flash all earth was left behind, and his soul was alone with God. It was a moment of absorbing joy, a ravishing spasm of comprehension, an earnest of eternal life, in which the philsopher-saint was unconscious even of those powers of the body by which his capacities for vision were sustained.

Such a silent and glorious meditation does not come to all men, nor would it satisfy every man's desire to worship. Man's worship is not a once-in-a-lifetime vision but a full-bodied adoration. We are directed to worship God in spirit and in truth, and truth to God and to His revela-

The Spirit of Glory

tion in the Incarnate Christ, as well as truth to the very nature of man's creation, demand an outward form, a spoken action, an uttered liturgy, a corporate sacrifice, in our worship of Almighty God.

In all experiences of human life, including all the highest acts of divine worship, the body and soul inevitably find expression together. When we look beyond this life to the great fulfillment of God's purpose for us hereafter, it is the "perfect consummation of bliss, both in body and soul" that we picture—a body, no longer a natural body, imperfect and sinful, but a spiritual body, completely responsive to the will of a soul made perfect in sanctification and holiness—body and soul alike reflecting the accomplishment of the Spirit of Glory.

[B]

The same principle—the use of outward means for the fulfillment of God's purpose—is revealed in the processes of nature. As we watch the development of a life, we see how God the Spirit nourishes the inward and hidden forces of life by outward processes which we can weigh and measure, which, with our growing knowledge, we can adopt and adjust to our needs. Consider a grain of corn: it is stored with the Spirit's precious gift of life; man cannot create it, nor can he give it life, but he can help it to grow or he can kill it. The seed may be hidden from light and water, denied its natural growth, and die; or the seed may be sown in a fair field where the rain can sprout it and the sun can warm it, and where it can lay hold of the richness of the soil and grow to an abundant harvest.

Sacrament

The sun, the rain, the cooling nights, and the warm earth and the farmer's cultivating care are all outward means by which a seed's hidden life is developed. It is God's way with nature; man has discovered that way, and, "thinking after God," has set himself to apply and develop the outward means which he himself has learned to control.

That is the normal way in nature; it is God's way. We know, however, that if it were the will of God, as in the feeding of the five thousand in the wilderness, God could develop life and bring it to maturity without the long process of secondary means; but that is not God's way. The Holy Spirit, the Giver of Life, works by outward means in developing the life which He has given. Men, as they learn the ways of the Spirit, may adapt the life which He gives, may regulate the form of its expression, may make new adjustments, may sift, select, combine, changing the fashion of the life according to their need, but the actual life itself remains God's gift. Man cannot create life; only God can do that, and it is God's secret. That inner principle, that unseen energy, that invisible power, God-given and God-sustained, is reproduced and multiplied in our midst by visible, outward means which the Spirit of Glory still directs.

The same principle of the Spirit's working by outward means is seen in the sphere of healing. The patient in the hospital will rightly attribute his cure to the medicine, the physician's skill, and the nurse's care, for they are all channels of the Spirit's healing. The medicine owes its virtue to some part of the mineral or vegetable world, where the Life-giver has been at work. It is the Spirit

The Spirit of Glory

under whose controlling care the development of surgical and medical knowledge has been made; it is the Spirit to whom the physician owes his marvellous skill; it is the Spirit from whom the nurse has won her patience, her knowledge, and her love. We know, however, that Jesus, if He willed, in the power of the Spirit, could heal at His word only, without any intermediary, without so much as the outward means of gesture, sign, or touch. Even so, as the normal way the Spirit heals and blesses by using outward secondary means—the means made familiar to us in ever-increasing miracles of medicine and surgery.

[C]

In the course of the revelation of God in the Old Testament a further step forward is taken in linking the Spirit's use of outward means with the fellowship, obedience, and conscious cooperation of man. God chooses outward means, simple and lowly in themselves, which, when set in motion by man's unhesitating obedience to the direct command of God, achieve results utterly incommensurate with the means employed.

After long years of sojourning in the wilderness the tribes of Israel found themselves facing the walled fortress of Jericho, guardian citadel of the Holy Land. They had no experience of siege warfare, and there was no other gate to the Promised Land. At that crisis the faith and obedience of Israel were put to the test by the command of Joshua. Once a day for six successive days the army of Israel marched around the walls of Jericho in silence, and on the seventh day seven times around; after

Sacrament

the blast of the trumpets and the horn and the great shout of the people, the walls of Jericho crumbled before their eyes and they walked victorious into the city. So God tested man's obedience. Where man obeys, there God, in His own way, gives success.

As they stood before Jericho, some of the Israelites might have recalled a similar trial of faith in the very midst of their wanderings. They had fallen amongst serpents, which bit the people and caused many of them to die. "And Moses made a serpent of brass, and put it upon a pole, and it came to pass that if a serpent had bitten any man, when he beheld the serpent of brass, he lived." It is the story of an act of implicit obedience used by God as an outward means by which the divine healing is imparted.

A more notable instance of the same principle is the cure of Naaman the leper—more notable, because it shows the struggle which Naaman had to wage with his own spirit of pride before he could accept such a lowly means of the divine healing, but the lesson is the same. No simpler means could be chosen than the bathing in the waters of Jordan. It involved a deliberate act of humility and obedience, and the magnitude of the result was totally incommensurate with the lowliness of the outward means employed.

In ways like that men of the Old Testament were prepared for the understanding of that fuller use of secondary and outward means, which the Spirit of God would employ when the Incarnation had become the measure of the capacity of earthly and material things and be the very channel by which God Himself approached man.

The Spirit of Glory
[D]

The Incarnation is the work of the Spirit of Glory and of God. Man had often thought that all things material must be essentially evil and could never be the vehicle of the revelation of God, but the world of matter was that very creation over which the Spirit of God Himself had brooded. It was essentially good, as God made it, but man had abused it and perverted it to evil uses. It was to be redeemed and rescued by the Spirit for the high purposes of God. "In the fullness of time," when there was no other pure lodgment upon the sinful world whereon the Holy Ghost might rest, Mary the Maid of Nazareth heard the words of the angel, "The Holy Ghost shall come upon thee, and the power of the Highest shall overshadow thee: therefore also that holy thing which shall be born of thee shall be called the Son of God."

In the fullness of time the Son of God was born, "and Jesus increased in wisdom and stature, and in favor with God and man." In the Spirit-guided life of Jesus we see the perfect pattern of a human life entirely responsive to the impulses of the indwelling Spirit of Glory; and all the while in the beauty of that life, which achieved so perfectly its high destiny, even through suffering and through death, God Himself was being disclosed. The incarnate life of Jesus was a sacrament of God, and so indeed may be any man's life. Our manhood, because it was made in the image of God, is a proper vehicle for the revelation of God. As people saw God in Christ, so may they see Him in us.

It was in the power of the Holy Spirit that Jesus "in-

Sacrament

creased in wisdom and stature, and in favor with God and man." When therefore at His Ascension Jesus withdrew Himself from human sight, He had no will to withdraw from man that source and spring of perfect human achievement, by whose guidance and indwelling His own human soul had accomplished the will of the Father; the Spirit of Glory, who had shaped and moulded "all the loveliness of that white life," was to be the new endowment offered to every human soul. He, who called and beckoned and taught and encouraged from without, was to dwell within the very souls of men, and guide them, sanctify them, and quicken them in the secret depths of their personal life. "He dwelleth with you, and shall be in you." It was the persistent purpose of Jesus to perpetuate the fruit of His holy life and atoning death among men by the mission of the Holy Ghost. He was to come as the Spirit of the Incarnate, sent forth out of the very heart of that sacred Humanity, which He had led from glory to glory until it was seated triumphant at the right hand of God.

So it was that the Holy Ghost revealed Himself as the Spirit of Grace, the minister of a risen yet ever-present Christ, the mediator of the glory of the Incarnate in human life, and all according to the divine promise, "We will come unto him, and make our abode with him." When love prepares the way by the simple use of the sacramental means, there Jesus manifests Himself. So the problem of Judas, "not Iscariot," is solved, "Lord, how is it that thou wilt manifest thyself unto us and not unto the world?" So necessarily and so intimately is the presence of the Spirit bound up with the work of Christ

The Spirit of Glory

among men that frequently St. Paul, in his short salutations, makes distinct mention only of the Father and the Son as the givers of that grace and peace which can come only through the sacramental agency of the Holy Spirit. It is the Spirit, who, by baptism brings us that first glory of union with God in the life of grace, which illuminates the mind, recreates the soul in the image of God, and imparts to it the character of holiness which befits a new member of the Church of God.

All this is not in itself a new work of the Holy Spirit; it is, however, effected in a new way, and operates more fully and surely. In the earlier training of Israel it was still the Holy Spirit to whom prophet, priest, and people alike owed their sanctification; but now the Incarnation has opened a new channel of access to God, and the gift of Pentecost marks out the new mission of the Spirit: He initiates each soul into the fellowship of Christ, not by the barren rite of circumcision, but the grace of the Holy Spirit's indwelling. This "heavenly washing" brings an everlasting benediction: Jesus, in the refounding of the Kingdom of God with ampler opportunity and fuller grace, receives us as the children of God, releases us of our sins, sanctifies us with the Holy Ghost, and gives us the kingdom of heaven and everlasting life. It is the Spirit who seals the soul with the stamp of God, that it may be secure against evil in the "ghostly strength" of His vital indwelling and that it may endure unto eternal life.

It remains true that the grace of God is not confined or limited to sacraments: God may still as in Old Testament days bestow grace where there is no sacrament; but for us the Incarnation, with its quickening of the

Sacrament

power of things material to subserve the spiritual, and its revelation of the lowliness and love of God, has created at once a new obligation, a new certainty, and a new hope. For us who love the Incarnate, sacrament is the way of faith. "Ye believe in God, believe also in me." God's way in the past had been the way of occasional inspiration, of individual sanctification, of unchartered grace; but now His way, revealed in His mission of the Spirit, is a settled order of holy fellowship, in which each member of His Church, through the sacrament of Baptism, is assured of the gift of divine sonship, divine pardon, sanctifying grace, mental illumination, and growing communion with God. Of the life that comes through sacrament the Spirit is both agent and source. It is natural therefore that He, who is God of Order, should Himself impart the special graces, inspirations, vocations, and impulses of His own bestowing through orderly channels called sacraments.

The Spirit bloweth indeed where He "listeth," but He has revealed where He wishes best to breathe: by the sacraments. By outward and visible means the Spirit of Glory and of God certifies His inspiration and His eternal indwelling. The person whose spiritual life made its beginning in the sacrament of Baptism finds in Confirmation, in Holy Communion, in Absolution, in Holy Unction, and, if it be his vocation, in Holy Orders or Holy Matrimony—in all the sacraments he finds the Holy Spirit using the same means—outward and visible signs—to assist and assure and inspire him in the path of Christian discipleship.

He, "unto whom all hearts are open, all desires known,

The Spirit of Glory

and from whom no secrets are hid," knows what we need and is careful to provide the order, security, and certainty upon which we may unfailingly rely when, with our changing moods and restless emotions, we seek fellowship with God and would fill our lives with the glory of the Eternal.

A PRAYER OF ADORATION

Holy Spirit of Life, Promise of the Father, Almighty God and Lord most High, we praise and bless thee for the ministries of thy sacramental grace, for the everlasting benediction of thy heavenly washing and the gift of eternal life, for the fruit of thy confirming grace, for the peace of Absolution, for the precious food of the Body and Blood of Jesus Christ our Lord, whereby we are filled with the fruits of his redemption. Praise be to thee for the life of the Church with all its covenanted blessings and for the countless mercies of thy boundless love. Accept our praise and keep us ever by thy power, most holy Paraclete, Spirit of Glory and of God. Amen.

IX

The Holy Eucharist

In the supreme sacrament of the altar, which crowns the hallowing work of the Spirit of Glory on earth, the Holy Ghost has a double office to perform: he prepares the Blessed Sacrament for man, and He prepares man for the Blessed Sacrament, and we dare not forget His holy work in either way. In no other manner does the Holy Spirit so closely touch our normal life of devotion.

[A]

The profound and glorious mystery of the Eucharist is the "Real Presence" of Jesus: it is the secret of its power, the source of its gladness, the pledge of its truth and efficacy; it is a presence of Jesus which the hallowing of the Spirit effects according to the will of God. It is to be remembered that human words must always be inadequate to express the glory of "such good things as pass man's understanding." Anyone who writes of the Holy Mysteries must speak the mind of the Church and with all sincerity pray the Holy Ghost that his words may bring light to some seeker after truth, and may not dim the bright certainty nor damp the ardor of any soul to whom God has revealed Himself in the fellowship of the

The Spirit of Glory

Holy Eucharist. Always our prayer must be "so to believe and to understand, to feel and firmly to hold, to speak and to think concerning so great a mystery as is well-pleasing to God and for the good of our souls."

In a celebration of the Holy Eucharist, the agent of the Holy Spirit is, of course, the priest, who, by divine calling, received from the Spirit himself the hallowing of ordination, with its tradition of apostolic authority and its personal consecration, so that in the Sacrifice of the Church he may both represent God to man and present man to God. Through the power of the Blessed Spirit of Glory and of God, the sacred words of our Lord's Institution are made effective to fulfill the declaration of Jesus Himself, and the same Spirit of Holiness who, in the bold phrase of St. Ambrose, was "the author of the Lord's Incarnation," now fulfills His work of glory in becoming the Minister of the sacramental presence of the same Incarnate Word.

Here are the words of the Liturgy of St. James, which the Church of Jerusalem used and which St. Cyril knew in the fourth century: "Have mercy upon us, O God, according to thy pity, and send down upon us and upon these gifts lying before thee, thy Spirit, the Lord and Life-Giver. Send down the same Spirit . . . upon us and upon these holy gifts lying before thee, that He may come upon them with His holy and good and glorious presence, and may hallow and make this bread to be the Holy Body of Christ and this cup the precious Blood of Christ. . . ." Similar words may be found in almost all the known liturgies of the East. The Liturgy of St. Chrysostom, which is in actual use in the

The Holy Eucharist

Orthodox Church of the East today, has these words: "Send down upon us and upon these gifts here set forth, thy co-eternal and consubstantial Holy Spirit, by whom blessing this bread thou wilt make it truly the Body of our Lord and Saviour Jesus Christ, and blessing this cup thou wilt make it really the Blood of our Lord and Saviour Jesus Christ, changing them by Thy Holy Spirit." The Western Liturgies have preserved nothing in their rites so full and explicit, but the Church of the West is at one with the Church of the East in its belief that the Holy Spirit is the actual agent of consecration in the Holy Mysteries.

It is He who effects the presence of the Incarnate Lord, according to Christ's promise, "He shall take of mine and shall show it unto you." In the Eucharist Jesus is present in the fullness of His created and now glorified humanity. It is the same humanity in which He trod the hills of Galilee, but our Lord's Body and Blood are not now as they were then: they exist now only in the condition or state of spiritual glory; and it is in that state that His Presence is manifested in the bread and the wine. It is in that state that He represents Himself for sacrifice, for communion, and for adoration. The sacramental presence of our Lord is the work of the Spirit; it is not the creation of our own minds, nor the product of our own devout imagination, but the gift of God. It does not depend on the faith of the communicant; it is not the fruit of our affection or spiritual desire; it is not merely the realization of spiritual truth, nor just the soul's quickened awareness of union with God: the presence of the Body and Blood of Jesus Christ is the glorious operation

The Spirit of Glory

of the Holy Ghost who works through the definitely appointed channel of human priesthood, and uses as His vehicle the creaturely elements of bread and wine.

How it is that the Spirit is able to use such earthly creatures for so glorious a purpose? What are the laws of the spiritual realm into which the hallowing work of the Holy Ghost carries us? That is a mystery—something utterly beyond our understanding. In proclaiming the fact of our Lord's eucharistic presence, we are not only relying upon the truth of our Lord's own words, we are not only at one with the experience of the most saintly lives of all the ages, who in this sacramental fellowship have found their most cherished and most fruitful communion with God, but we have also our own personal knowledge of the spiritual realities of union with Jesus, and of the communication of His life, which we ourselves have found in the "Breaking of the Bread." There is true insight in the experience of the exact theologian of the sixteenth century who said, "What these elements are in themselves it skilleth not. It is enough that to me which take them they are the Body and Blood of Christ. His promise is sufficient. . . . He knoweth which way to accomplish. . . . O my Lord, Thou art true; O my soul, thou art happy."

When we do try for some fuller understanding of the way of the Holy Spirit in assuring us of the sacramental presence of Jesus, we are helped by recalling the Spirit's work in preparing the human nature for the earthly mission of the Incarnate Lord. The Word made flesh, and dwelling among us was not just a manifestation of the omnipresence of God: it was a definite presence of God under the

The Holy Eucharist

peculiar limitations of a creaturely existence. So the sacramental presence of Jesus is not just a particular moment of His omnipresence as God, but a glorious experience of His Incarnate Life.

It is not difficult to see the marks which distinguish Christ's omnipresence from His sacramental presence. As Eternal God, Jesus is always and everywhere present: equally with the Father and the Holy Ghost, Jesus has been ever present to every creature ever since the beginning of time. In God we live and move and have our being. We are ever in the presence of the Eternal Word, who is one with the Father and the Holy Ghost in the undivided glory of God. He is the life of all that lives. Wherever I am, wherever I place myself, I am equally and in the same way within the sphere of God's omnipresence. It depends upon myself and my own will and concentration as to how far I am able to recognize that presence. When at the beginning of my prayer, I say, "Let me put myself in the presence of God," it is an appeal to myself to gather together all my powers of mind and soul, that I may be conscious of that presence in which I am always living. The presence is there, and I am sustained by it, whether I acknowledge God or forget Him. I bring myself into the direct realization of His presence by my own individual effort, just as I open my eyes to see the sunrise.

The fulfillment of Christ's promise, "Where two or three are gathered together in my name, there am I in the midst of them," is a revelation of His presence under certain definite conditions. It is the presence of Christ recognized by those who are members of His Body,

The Spirit of Glory

acting in obedience to His will, and consciously putting themselves at the disposal of His loving purposes. Furthermore, it is a presence which is manifested in such a form that it cannot actually make entrance into the soul without man's personal response and appropriation.

The gift which the Holy Spirit prepares in the Eucharist is characteristic of that sacrament alone. It is the Body and Blood of Christ given to us in the fullness of His humanity according to the mode of His creaturely nature now risen and glorified; of that we can actually partake, and for that we have been made ready by the indwelling of the Holy Spirit. The gift of the sacramental presence of the Incarnate can be appropriated by us in the innermost depths of our personality and it can effect body and soul alike. This is the Spirit's great work of glory in the Sacrament, "He shall glorify me: for he shall receive of mine, and shall show it unto you." The Holy Spirit takes the outward, creaturely, material gifts of bread and wine, makes them the vehicle of the presence of Jesus. The gift is spiritual, because the glorified human nature of Christ is now spiritual; it is real, because He is reality Himself; it is sacramental, because the outward and visible forms of bread and wine are not desstroyed; and finally it is ineffable, because no words of ours can fitly describe the glory, the reality, the eternity of heavenly things.

There will always be some minds which will seek to probe the way of the Spirit more closely: aware that it is the proper sphere of the Holy Ghost to penetrate material things and to make the material world subserve a higher

The Holy Eucharist

order, they are restless until they can find some recognized principle which offers at least some approach towards an acceptable explanation of the Spirit's action. Perhaps for such minds it may be in the realm of the philosophy of reality that the most helpful guidance may be found. There are grades of reality—matter, life, mind, spirit— and each finds its perfection only in relation to something else, something higher than itself. For us, in our condition of existence, there is no such thing as "pure" matter, "pure" life, "pure" mind, "pure" spirit (only God is pure Spirit, but here we are talking about the natural things of this life), and each much be considered in relation to something else.

The bread which we offer in the Eucharist is real—real in that it possesses a reality endowed by, enclosed in, and limited to nature: we can see it, touch it, smell it, and taste it; for us, in our state of existence, that bread *is*. Plain bread, however, is without ultimate reality—it is not "really real;" but by the consecrating power of the eternal Spirit of Glory the bread we offer is made so—made "really real": it is endowed by and enclosed within the absolute, the ultimate, the eternal; the imperfect reality of the earthly and material creature is taken into and supported by a greater reality: God Himself—Reality utterly beyond the apprehension of our finite senses. The Sacrament is appropriate to the needs of our human nature; it is a visible and tangible pledge and assurance of that fellowship with God which is the promised work of the Holy Spirit. Thus the Spirit achieves His work as the minister of the living Christ: He brings us to Jesus

The Spirit of Glory

and Jesus to us in an act of sacred and intimate communion. The prayer of the Lady Julian is answered, "God of Thy goodness, give me Thyself. If I ask anything else, ever me wanteth."

[B]

How shall we prepare ourselves to come into this Presence? It is the work of the Holy Spirit to lead us to Jesus; only in conscious response to His leading can we be assured of the right temper of approach. He begins His work in us by giving us the longing for Jesus. Our frequent mistake is to think that we can create that desire ourselves. That is why our devotion is often so spasmodic, so obviously a matter of external rule, so much a thing of convention, so seldom a joyous inspiration, so wanting in naturalness and freedom. Only he who is already drinking of the water-brooks of the Spirit, can say, "My soul is athirst for God, yea, even for the living God: when shall I come to appear before the presence of God?" We know by the soul's experience of hunger that life without God is death, for we sometimes have that sense at moments of spiritual crisis. The longing for God is not reserved for the ecstatic soul, which in moments of rapture is borne into spiritual realms never enjoyed by ordinary Christians; it is the source of all devotion in the life of every Christian. It is the Spirit who gives us the longing, who gives us the vision of God. It is He also who rouses the soul to long for the vision and sustains the effort needed to attain it. The first preparation for our Eucharist is to pray to the Holy Ghost to quicken

The Holy Eucharist

our desire for God. We must really seek God and know that without Him we are desolate, powerless, inefficient, and incomplete.

That is the beginning of our real preparation. It is not enough to be interested in our own souls, to be regular in practices of devotion, to be scrupulous in habits of discipline; we must want God. Religiosity is not religion. Religion is life; it is work, a living quest, a living loyalty, a living fellowship, a glorious achievement—all wrought in the power of God. Religiosity is play—play with vital impulses, abuse of spiritual powers, self-deceiving, self-destroying. Religion braces the soul to do work for God, to extend His kingdom to bear brave witness, to venture all for Christ's sake. Religiosity is concerned with feelings, emotions, and spiritual comforts.

The whole purpose of the Eucharistic gift is to strengthen us for the normal duties of life, to make us actual Christ-bearers as we move out into the world, to make perfect our obedience, to equip us with strength for our tasks, to inspire us as we set ourselves to do Christ's work. Of all people, it is the communicant who should be foremost in the great social efforts and public duties and endeavors after righteousness, justice, and truth. Is this actually our conception of the grace we seek in the Eucharist? Is it the strength by which all our work is done? Or is it only a spiritual luxury, a refinement of devotional life, a mark of loyalty to the Church, a courteous respect for her teaching and discipline?

The Spirit-given grace not used is a lacking grace. Therefore, we must ask the Holy Spirit to make it clear to us that there is a work in the world which only God

The Spirit of Glory

can do, and that we are the ones through whom God wants to work. Can we not be thrilled with the hope and joy of being God's worker? Think of the wonder of the act by which God deigns to continue to us in the Eucharist the opportunity of fellowship with the Incarnate Saviour! Have a mind that the high purpose of God shall not be frustrated. Make a fresh act of faith in the love of God which brings Jesus so near. Renew that simple act of faith at each approach to the altar. Remember that it is Jesus Himself who comes to you. Respond with the will and intention to work and witness for God in the power of the Holy Ghost. Make your act of will as definite and explicit as the leading of the Spirit may direct.

There are, of course, other natural and accustomed avenues of devotion: there are acts of penitence, humility and love, and an earnest effort of recollection as we gather all our powers together for a new act of worship. Again and again, however, there is distress because in these days, when time is short and work falls so much more heavily upon those who used to count upon hours of leisure, it seems impossible to find sufficient time to prepare for our communion. Perhaps it is God's way of reminding us that work is part of our devotion, and that duty is part of our sacrifice to God. Certainly it sets a higher dignity upon our work, it touches our work more brightly with the glory of perfection, if we can feel that today's tasks are really part of our actual preparation for our next communion. It is so easy to divorce our communion from the daily conduct of our common life. It is a happy thing

The Holy Eucharist

to be able conscientiously to relate the simple drudgeries of the day, the normal duties of the hour, and all the monotonies of life, to the glory of the altar and to see in them God's own appointed way of approach to fellowship with Jesus.

If that hope of fresh communion with Jesus can be the inspiration of our work, then, as we add task to task, we are making a worthy approach and completing a sufficient preparation; then the Holy Spirit is indeed guiding us to a complete offering of our souls and bodies as a reasonable, holy, and living sacrifice; and when the hour of communion draws near and we kneel for our last moments of preparation, it is short work to make a recollected act of penitence, oblation, and intention, in which all the living energies of our present self are gathered up into real and full expression. We shall not need the words of others to guide us: we can speak for ourselves. The Spirit of Glory, who has blessed us in our work, will quicken our memories, kindle our hearts, and preserve our minds from distraction, and bring us humble, expectant, and sincere into the joyous Presence of Jesus.

[C]

If we can regard the work of our daily life as a preparation for communion, so also in our daily work can our thanksgiving after communion find its truest expression. In the hush of the quiet church we may have a little time for worship, for recollection, for thanksgiving, for renewal of purpose, but never so much time as we would

The Spirit of Glory

wish; home duties call and the service of others claims us. We must rise and go, but we do not go alone. Not only have we the renewed memory of Jesus, but we have the renewed grace of His Presence. Christ is with us. His great gift of grace has re-created us. Our real thanksgiving will be expressed by stirring up that gift to new exercise, to making loyal use of that new strength, in the duties that lie immediately before us. "I can do all things through Christ which strengtheneth me." Here is the strength of Christ newly given to me: it must be used and displayed. Our thanksgiving does not end as the church door closes upon us; indeed that is when it really begins. The first person we meet ought to meet Christ in us. If that is the spirit in which we thank God for His fellowship, God's strength will never fail us. We shall be equal to our tasks. The tasks themselves will be transfigured. The sense of duty, that has hardly been able to drag us to our work, will be lost in the glad response of the soul to the sufficiency of God we received in the Eucharist. Such a thanksgiving is a pledge of progress. God gives "grace for grace." For as the condition of a higher call of God is the fulfillment of His first vocation, so our surest preparation for new grace is the constant use of grace already given.

A PRAYER BEFORE COMMUNION

O Holy Ghost, Giver of Life and Font of Sanctity, who by thy consecrating power dost change the shadows of earthly things into the realities of the Body and Blood of Christ and dost show to us the things of Jesus; Have mercy upon us, that with pure affection and a clean heart

The Holy Eucharist

we may receive our Lord and God, and by works of holiness manifest him openly in our lives, who liveth and reigneth with thee and the Father, one God, world without end. Amen.

X

Ministry

As the Spirit of Glory inspired the life-work of Him who came not to be ministered unto but to minister, and as the Holy Spirit is the minister of the Incarnate Lord in His present mission to men, so it is the same Spirit who equips men perfectly for their manifold ministries today. The supreme glory of ministry is priesthood. The word priest grates on some ears and is suspect in some circles. To a superficial and self-loving age, priestliness can never be congenial, and even among religious people a priest is often misunderstood and sadly vilified; but to every noble conception of human life priestliness is essential. Through the long ages of the world's history there has been no religion which has not treasured some ideal of priesthood and sacrifice, however vague and shadowy; but we today have no need to deal with shadows, for we have before us the supreme and perfect priesthood of Jesus, our Incarnate and Ascended Lord.

[A]

There are three ideas which all priesthood seeks in general to express: first, the sense of man's disability or impotence in the face of God; secondly, the consciousness

Ministry

of the need of sacrifice, culminating in the offering of life itself; and, lastly, the realization of fellowship and communion with God as the true end and purpose of man.

With each of these ideas the high-priesthood of Jesus has intimate relations and flashes upon each the revealing light of eternal truth.

The sense of disability in the face of God, the consciousness of weakness and infirmity, Jesus Himself accepted fully when He became man. He entered into all the limitations of man's finite nature. No one ever expressed more completely man's essential dependence upon God. Out of the heart of a creaturely manhood, holy, harmless, and undefiled, rose the priesthood of Jesus.

The truly human instinct to offer life itself as the only sacrifice really worthy of God was fulfilled by the offering of Christ upon the Cross. His offering was not a symbolic one, of bulls or goats; He brought no substitute, no representative; rather He offered Himself in the perfect fullness of His ideal manhood, an entire dedication, without blemish, without reserve—a life surrendered at every point, that passed under the harrow of the Passion, through the agony of death upon the Cross—not a momentary, but a constant offering. He lives as sacrifice as well as priest. His ascended life is a perpetual offering. In Him manhood stands offered and accepted before the throne of God.

Since the end of all priestly work is fellowship with God, Jesus brings the long development of man to rest in God. His sacrifice becomes our peace. That life which He brought victoriously through death is not only offered

The Spirit of Glory

perpetually in the courts of heaven and pleaded constantly on the altars of His Church on earth, but it is also imparted to us in sacraments which He has lovingly devised. Jesus fulfills all priesthood and mediates to us that endless life which is the goal of human destiny—eternal fellowship with God. By Him, through Him, and with Him we dwell in God, and He in us.

[B]

The priesthood of Jesus links man with God, and with that priesthood His mystical body, the Church, is identified. It is the lesson of the Gospels that it was the will of Jesus that the work which He began should be fulfilled and achieved through the Church in the power of the Spirit. The work of His priesthood, begun on earth and continued in heaven, is shared by us who are gathered into His Church. The Church is essentially a priestly body, "a royal priesthood," "a holy priesthood," in God-given ways mediating the grace and truth of Jesus to the world for whose salvation it lives and works.

It is natural that the Church as a great and divine society should express its corporate functions through definite organs, and in so doing it is subject to the same needs as the civil body, the State. The body politic must have its chosen organs—the judiciary, the armed forces, the civil service—not to deprive people of their civic rights, but to safeguard them, to ensure that each has his due share of the rights of citizenship. Through such special agents the corporate activities of the State are carried on. Nor is it within the power of any of us to appoint

Ministry

ourselves to any office in the same, when or as we will.

The Church has its appointed agents—bishops, priests, and deacons, who, in one way or another, exercise the ministry of the Body of Christ. They fulfill their functions, not as organs of this or that congregation, but as ministers of the whole Catholic Church of Christ. They do not choose themselves: they are chosen of God. They are conscious of the inward call of the Spirit. The faithful give witness of their character and approve them worthy of such a trust. The bishops in the name and in the power of Christ become the channels and pledge of their divine acceptance. Through the laying on of a bishop's hands they receive the authority of Christ to execute their office in the Church of God, and are endowed with the power of the Holy Spirit for the sanctification of their lives and to make them worthy of their calling. Their priesthood is a ministerial priesthood. They are stewards of God, dealing faithfully and securely with divine gifts, originating nothing themselves, but mediating the mercy and bounty, yea, the very Presence of God Himself. They carry on in the life of grace the work of human mediation which began when Jesus became man, which He Himself committed to the Apostles, and which the Holy Ghost has handed down to us through the ages in the unity of the Church of God.

[C]

The fulfillment of ministerial priesthood in no way deprives any member of the Body of his personal priesthood, his own individual priestly responsibilities. The

The Spirit of Glory

priesthood of the believer, which comes to its maturity in the gift of Confirmation, is no shallow phrase, no empty dignity: it is a real vocation, a high mission, an ordination to a fruitful ministry of unselfish service in the name and power of Christ; it fulfills itself along the very lines of service of which we have been thinking.

The priesthood of the believer takes root in a sense of personal infirmity, in a realization of the magnificence of God before whom that person stands. The sense of natural disability is quickened by the consciousness of sin. It is to us in our sin-stricken weakness that God reveals Himself as love, mighty to save. It is out of our very weakness that we build up our personal faith and rest securely in the atoning merits of the sinless Redeemer. It is out of the knowledge of our own infirmity that we glory in the cleansing power of the Precious Blood, and commit ourselves to Jesus as Friend and Saviour, and learn to use fully the freedom of prayer, the individual access to the throne of grace, which the victory of Christ has won. So all our Godward life is touched with the glory of a great humility, the very lowliness of which is our strength. It is no longer our weakness that confounds us at every step, but the majesty and the love of God that casts an aura of sanctity about every movement of our life.

In the exercise of the privilege of access to God in prayer we see the Lord high and lifted up, and steep ourselves in the magnificence, the majesty, and the splendor of God. We see life everywhere aglow with God. In the light of that vision we take up our burdens, we meet our duties, we bear our witness. Insensibly there

Ministry

passes into our lives that spirit of happiness and joy which is a reflection of the Glory of God shining through our lives. We move out to our tasks with that simple serenity, unaffected, unafraid and unoppressed, which is the birthright of the children of God.

The second mark of our priestliness as believers is offering sacrifice. It is not for us, as it is for the ministerial priesthood, to offer sacrifice on behalf of the whole Body, but it is for us to make that corporate offering effective by presenting our own lives under the cover of that sinless offering which is pleaded in the great Eucharistic Sacrifice upon our earthly altars. Always we have ourselves to offer; nothing less will ever satisfy our need, no external gifts, however costly, but just ourselves. We learn, we train and discipline ourselves, we grow rich in knowledge and experience, that we may have more and more to offer. All through our lives our personal gifts and individual talents, our knowledge and our skill, are held in stewardship for the help and happiness of others. The supreme glory of our priesthood is that, being already "accepted in the Beloved," we bring our redeemed life with all its saving powers to help in the redeeming work of Christ in His Church. Our "royal priesthood" is just this—succor, service, sacrifice, personal mediation on behalf of a world that languishes apart from Christ. To learn the ways of ministry in the power of the Spirit is to know that sacrifice and service are the true measures of life's happiness, and to realize that if ever we fall into ways of selfishness and forget the common good in sloth, self-pity or self-indulgence, we are false to the most treasured traditions of our spiritual heritage.

The Spirit of Glory

As the end of all priesthood is communion with God, so the priesthood of the believer realizes itself in happy recourse to the sacramental fellowship which is the crown of the Spirit's ministry. It is for that reason that we treasure so dearly and safeguard so carefully the ministerial priesthood. It is not that the priest comes between the soul and God; rather we know that never is the soul so closely held in the grip of God; never do we come into such close touch with the radiant personality of Jesus Himself, as when the priest is fulfilling his office at the altar. It is then that Jesus, our Friend, our Saviour, and our King, meets us: He dwells in us and we in Him. Amid the duties of each day, we learn to stay our hearts on God, we enter into the mind of Christ and find strength to do His will, and our lives open out in the glory of His presence. It is to this that the Spirit of Glory and of God leads us; it is in this that we make full proof of our ministry and respond to His vocation. Caught by the vision of a God who ministers to us with such munificence, we lose ourselves in ministering royally to others, and we find strength for that ministry in ever-deepening fellowship with Him who "came not to be ministered unto, but to minister, and to give his life a ransom for many." So we grow strong in our "royal" and "holy priesthood," finding its beauty and splendor solely at its source, God Himself.

A PRAYER FOR SERVICE

Blessed Spirit of God, who dost call men and angels to the service of the Lord most high; Stir in our hearts the

Ministry

love of Jesus, that loving all for his sake we may be made worthy by thy grace to take part in the redemptive work of his kingdom, and yielding ourselves to his obedience may follow gladly where he calls and set forth the cause of righteousness and peace through all the world in the fellowship of thy holy Church; through the same Jesus Christ our Lord and Saviour. Amen.

XI

Fellowship

"How shall not the ministration of the spirit be rather glorious?" is the thought of St. Paul when he is contrasting the glory of the Christian life ministered by "the Spirit of the living God" to the old Jewish dispensation which he describes as a "ministration of death, written and engraven in stones." Perhaps the supreme mark of Christian glory in human life is the fellowship which the Spirit creates. God is fellowship. That is the meaning of the Holy Trinity. Man is made for fellowship. The fellowship which he seeks with his brethren can be ensured only by the fellowship with God, which is the work of the Spirit.

We know today far better than we did a few years ago that man can attain his true development only in the society of and dealings with his fellows. This has been dimly apprehended through all the ages, when the wisest philosophers and statesmen have tried to frame a society that shall be a stable and firm bond of fellowship between men, a society which shall know neither the limitations and hindrances of distance nor of time. All failed because the foundation was not laid in God. Only the Society which the Spirit founded in the fellowship of Jesus could have in it the promise of eternity. The Church of God

Fellowship

stands firm as the fellowship which fulfills the hopes of men in all ages and in all climes: it is, as St. Paul summarily describes it, a fellowship "in Christ." The history of the Church has developed the marks of that fellowship, and has shown the strength of those bonds of the Spirit's making which have drawn together and kept together men of goodwill and character and vision through all the ages. The ministration of the Spirit in the Church realizes a fellowship in life, in faith, and in worship—a fellowship which offers to man the fulfillment of all his highest hopes and greatest glory.

[A]

The fellowship of the Holy Spirit realizes itself first in community of life. Primarily and essentially the Christian religion is a corporate life, lived under the banner of love. Though men may see in it a system, a philosophy, a doctrine, an institution, Christianity is first and last and always a life—not just a way, but a life. It affects every part of our daily work: it issues in conduct, it creates character, it manifests comradeship. The Catholic religion shows itself achieved and perfected, not in its doctrinal statements, not in its sacramental certainties, not in its ordered rites and ceremonies, but in its manifestation of a corporate life, rich in all the fruits of love, and wide as the world in its embrace.

It was so in the early days, when the Spirit of Glory distinguished the infant Church with such unfailing marks of abounding vitality and such signal evidences of corporate unity and vigor. The Christian life revealed

The Spirit of Glory

certain great traits of character which Roman and Greek alike envied, but could not attain. Christians disclosed a singular integrity of character, a goodness, a moral purity, which evinced a new ideal of restraint and self-discipline. They were indeed men of like passions with their fellows, but they bridled their passions, they curbed their selfish desires, they kept themselves from the sins of avarice and immorality which were eating out the life of the old world. They presented in a compact and harmonious unity a social vigor and personal chastity which were the very salt of civilization.

By living so, they did not live to themselves. In the midst of a hostile world, they set a new standard of active kindliness, benevolence, and love. It was not only that they loved one another and could not exhaust the mutual duties of loving-kindness towards their fellow Christians, but they abounded in ministries of self-sacrifice and service towards others. They thought, they worked, they lived, in terms of fellowship and love. Their love, their self-sacrificing, their dedication, their response to the needs of the poor, the feeble, and the enslaved—all was undeniable witness of fellowship in the life of the Catholic Church.

Their love was no weak thing: it was the enrichment of all the powers of life in the fulfillment of one supreme devotion. All the loyalties of life were merged in surrender to Jesus as King. That was what the heathen world noticed most of all. With all its ways of gentleness and peace, the Christian life showed a virility of purpose, a vitality of power, an irresistible strength, which wrested

Fellowship

triumph out of defeat. There was an unconquerable gladness, an exultation of heart, an inner assurance, which gave a steadfast dignity to human life, and which no persecution could break down. The Christian had access to springs of energy and life which made him victor over every foe. That life drew its strength from fellowship with God. Its energies were the inrush of heavenly forces into human life, its activities were the outgoings of divine holiness, drawn by sacramental channels from God Himself.

That is the fellowship of life which we today must hold fast in the power of the Spirit—a life of love. Love in the Catholic Church is not a sentiment, but a service; not an ecstasy, but an agony of sacrifice. Such love can be shed abroad in our hearts only by the Holy Spirit: there we must seek it—in the very heart of God. The energies of that love are not absorbed in the contemplation of God: they derive their force, their constancy from the love of God, but they flow out in manifold ministries of service towards our fellows. The challenge of the Beloved Disciple rings true and clear, "He that loveth not his brother whom he hath seen, how can he love God whom he hath not seen?" That is the end, that is the test, of all our Christian principles, our Catholic devotion, our ritual, and our Creed. They all must issue in a life of active love—a love that makes us think kindly, speak kindly, and act kindly, and see Jesus Himself in those whom we least understand, and address ourselves to them with reverent and real humility, with gentle patience and an inexhaustible faith in their power to respond to the

The Spirit of Glory

promptings of the Spirit of God. We shall love Jesus in them, for, as Bosseut says, "In the love of Jesus is born an immense love of souls."

All the great world problems today, problems of national rivalry, of race, of class, of industry, of labor, of education, of poverty—all can be finally solved only where the fellowship of life in God is found. We do not have to wait for the Church to organize some great scheme nor for any Church assembly to define for us the limits of our sacrifice: we have only to offer personal holiness, personal sacrifice, and personal sympathy, and give not according to man's quota but according to God's needs. The apostolate of love is the fruit of Church fellowship. All the powers and all the responsibilities of our corporate life lead out to this, and it will be by such a Spirit-born witness that the glory of fellowship in the Catholic Church of God will be vindicated by us today in the midst of a harassed and dizzy world.

[B]

The first glory of the Spirit's ministration in the Church is its fellowship of Life in God; the second glory is its fellowship in faith. The more you realize the constraint and the beauty of the Christian life of love, the more you are driven to ask, what sustains it? What protects it? Behind such a life stands a sure conviction, a reasoned faith, a certain knowledge. There can be no abiding enthusiasm for the life of love and fellowship, no satisfaction for our deepest instincts of corporate service, without a steadfast belief in God. The distinctive glory of the Christian faith

Fellowship

is that our knowledge of God is based not on speculation, but upon actual facts—actual events in the history of the world. The Incarnation of Jesus Christ is, of course, the supreme disclosure of God, made known to us in our day by the Church of History and recorded in the Gospels—facts which belong to the very events of our own experience today. It is an historic fact that Jesus, the Son of God, became man at Bethlehem for love of us and for our salvation. It is an historic fact that He died upon the Cross in the days of Pontius Pilate. That He rose from the dead, that He ascended into heaven to prepare a place for us, that He sent forth the Holy Spirit to prepare us for the place which He had won, that He gathered men into His Church, in order that they might find fellowship with God, and grace and truth and life eternal—they are all facts upon which the fellowship of our faith is founded.

Those facts are enshrined in the Creed, which from the first century has been the watchword and rallying cry of the faithful of the Church of the New Testament. The Church rescued those facts from oblivion, put them in the Creed, and safeguards them from misunderstanding and perversion. Before ever the Gospels were written, those facts were taught by the Apostles and confessed by the believing Church. Through the long ages of the Church's history, all its sacrifices, all its energy, all its authority and power, have been directed to the preservation of those facts and the fearless proclamation of their truth and meaning. The great value of the Church's Creed is that it does not present to us subtle inferences, nor probabilities, but simple, historic facts. It recalls to us the

The Spirit of Glory

sublime figure of the historic Christ, the Divine Redeemer, the Eternal God, and challenges us to accept in all their simple greatness the facts of God's revelation in Christ.

The Creed is no academic symbol, no mere exercise in theology, but a statement of faith that is worked into the very texture of life. It is there, in its application to the facts of our daily life, that it justifies itself. We hold it fast, not by intellectual assent, but by living it out in every deed.

Is God almighty? Then life has a purpose, and every day its work. Is He our Father? Then we may rest secure in His love and live safely under His protecting care. Did God become man? Then human life has a dignity worthy of heaven, and in the lowliest ways of life we can find God. Jesus suffered and died for us; therefore we know that sin is evil, and suffering may glow with the benediction of God. Jesus rose from the dead; therefore we can have fellowship with God and abiding union with one another, and the Church in the power of the Spirit has opened its arms to receive us into its eternal brotherhood in Christ. This is the fellowship of faith, which sustains our corporate life of love. "This is the victory that overcometh the world, even our faith. Who is he that overcometh the world, but he that believeth that Jesus is the Son of God?"

It is to sure facts, unquestionable certainties, that Scripture and tradition and the experience of the ages all bear witness; it is upon facts that the fellowship of the Church's life is solidly built.

Fellowship

[C]

As we realize the part which the Holy Spirit of Fellowship plays, both in the shaping and the interpreting of the Faith of the Church, two duties break upon us: We must study the Faith and we must live by it.

The Faith of the Church is so sublime that its implications can never be exhausted by the profoundest human thought, yet it is so simple that it can be grasped by the least instructed. It is the glory of the Spirit to guide us into all truth, both corporately and individually. The Spirit guides the Church collective, as its history has proved, and preserves it from error and misunderstanding. He also guides the mind and enlightens the conscience of the individual. It is true indeed that in the heart and life, rather than in the mind, the Christian faith finds its most general vindication; it is also true, as it has been said, that God accepts the faith of the charcoal burner, that is, the faith that questions nothing. Yes, God indeed accepts and enjoys the simple faith of the charcoal burner, but how few of us are charcoal burners? We are not peasants, but men and women of a certain education, who exercise trained thought and care in all the duties and business of life. The Spirit of Glory challenges us not to rule out religion from the sphere of our mental interest and intellectual activities, but to make a constant effort to "bring into captivity every thought to the obedience of Christ."

It is seldom that we bring our best faculties of thought to bear upon the truth of our religion, yet we can hardly

The Spirit of Glory

take an active and effectual interest in any subject of which we have only a superficial knowledge. Today many doors once closed stand open and reveal to us new discoveries, new tendencies of thought, science, and philosophy, fresh methods of intellectual approach—all of which throw new light on the revelation of God; they confirm from so many different sides the fundamental truths of the Faith, they test the reality of our belief, and enlarge our religious life with a new relation to the thought and activity of the modern world. It is not the learning of the expert, but the disciplined study, the intellectual effort of the ordinary thinking man and woman, that we need. The expert may prove one-sided, pedantic, remote from the normal experiences of workaday life; his theories have to be corrected or confirmed by the facts of spiritual experience; his theology may need the revealing light of true religion. The sincere and earnest follower of Christ Crucified has his own contribution to make to the corporate understanding of the Creed by offering his own living interpretation of the faith which he has received from the Spirit in response to his eager effort of thought and study. Thus it is that we find mutual support and encouragement in the fellowship of faith.

The second duty is to conform our daily life to the rule of faith. The Creed is not a mere recital of past facts, but the proclamation of a living Lord, to whose love we are making daily response. We confess our appeal to the risen Christ who has caught us up into the energies of His own divine life. To say of the Creed is to avow a personal surrender to the love of Jesus and to confess a growing experience of fellowship with God. The Spirit

Fellowship

of Glory will teach us that there is never such a thing as a mere repetition of the Creed. As we say it day by day, it is always new, always fresh, always aglow with new meaning. I cannot say the Creed today quite as I said it yesterday. It will mean more for me today in proportion as "I have set God always before me" yesterday. The experience of ruling life by the guidance of the Creed yesterday has given me today a deeper understanding, a firmer grasp, a fuller reliance, and a fresher interpretation of its truth. Each day I make progress in the fellowship of faith, and the Creed becomes inwoven into my life. It guides me in my daily intercourse with God, and I enter into fellowship of life and thought with all those men of faith and holy desire, who through the ages have added by their own constant experience to the wealth and beauty of the Christian life. The Spirit of Glory and of God resting upon us has made us one in loyalty and hope and love.

[D]

Fellowship of faith issues in fellowship of worship. The Spirit of Glory who gives wisdom, knowledge, and understanding enriches us also with the gift of holy fear. Adoration is the response of the soul to the majesty and mystery of God; without it there can be learning, but not wisdom; there may be genius, but not character. We see it in the innocent wonder of the child, the eager hero-worship of youth, the ecstacy of the heart in its first love of God, or the tranquil assurance of the soul that has plumbed the deepest secrets of prayer. These are the ways

The Spirit of Glory

in which the ministration of the Spirit is "rather glorious" as the soul comes face to face with the glory of Eternal Truth.

The altar of the Church is the school of adoration, and the apprehension of God is the measure of our worship. God is no less reverenced in the homeliness of His intimacy than in the majesty of His transcendent glory; but even in the most ecstatic moments of our adoring contemplation, it is not the worship of a lonely soul that we offer, but the worship of a soul linked in an eternal bond of fellowship with the redeemed of every age; it is the worship of the Church, uplifting, soaring, supremely sacrificial, representing mankind at its best and highest, in its moments of nearest access to God. It is something to be learned, studied, and treasured—a hallowed inheritance. If it is to be worthy of a God so glorious, vouchsafing His very Presence to us here, shining through the veil of sacrament, if it is to honor a God, who by the very gift of the Incarnation has raised earthly things to be the symbol and the channel of the eternal, can any earthly worship be too splendid in its beauty, too stately in its dignity, to express the fullness of man's homage? It is in hushed worship before the altar that we find and hold that spirit of awed reverence, that all-surrendered adoration, that constant sense of the solemn wonder of God's presence in His holy Church.

The distinctive mark of Christian worship is the spirit of never-ceasing penitence; it is the humble adoration of those who know themselves to be redeemed, who know that they have washed their robes and made them white in Blood of the Lamb.

Fellowship

The sanctuary is the place where the worship of the redeemed finds radiant expression in the beauty of holiness, and the altar is the school of adoration, but we should be wrong if we thought that the sanctuary of the house of God was the only, or even the most frequent, or most important, place where the light of Christian reverence shines. It is born at the font; it is renewed and rekindled at the altar; but its rays are as wide as human life. It is this spirit of adoration, sensitive to the transfiguring majesty of the presence of Jesus, and in whatever other ways He may appear, that makes the common day beautiful with the tender graces, the dear courtesies of love. The ingrained good manners of daily life, its chivalries, its loyalties, its "please" and its "thank you,"—the kind look, the gentle deference, the instinctive sympathy, the joy in all that is beautiful in human nature and good in human life—what are all these but fruit of the adoring soul that worships the Incarnate Christ? For us who believe in that Incarnate Love, adoration opens the gate of a new world and reveals a new glory in human life. We go forth from the altar, moving as worshippers in a new world, where the very silence speaks of God, and every sound is but the herald of His holy Name.

Thus it is that the Spirit of Glory reveals to us new depths of fellowship with the whole world—with one another, and with God. We must hold fast our worship, if we would keep the springs of life fresh and clear; we must hold fast our faith, if we would take our part in that promised victory that overcomes the world; we must hold fast our life of holiness and love, if we would commend the faith of Christ to our age—and to generations

The Spirit of Glory

yet to come. We will hold fast the fellowship of the Holy Spirit, not merely in order to have a crown to cast before the Redeemer's throne, but because it is the way in which the Spirit of Glory inspires and empowers us to set forward the coming of Christ's kingdom and to be worthy of our great and holy calling.

AN ACT OF ADORATION

O Holy Ghost, Lord and Giver of Life, Spirit of Righteousness and Grace, we adore thee and praise thee for the beauty of life, for the glory of man, for the quickening of our minds and the kindling of our hearts, for thy gracious indwelling and the hallowing of earthly things, and for the revelation of Jesus Christ. Grant to us ever thankful hearts that we may not misuse thy gifts nor forget thy bounty; and bring us, we pray, in peace and safety to God our hope and our Redeemer, that in him we may find rest and everlasting life; through the mediation of Jesus Christ, our Saviour and our King. Amen.

Cathedral of St. James Library
South Bend, Indiana